DIVINICUS

rise of the divine human

by Open

Openhand Press

DIVINICUS: rise of the divine human
by Open, Openhand Foundation

First edition: printed 1st September 2014
Published by Openhand Press

ISBN 978-0-9556792-3-0

Cover design: Trinity Bourne

for Trinity and her Angels,
my supportive grace

Contents

Foreword

I had to hit the ground running. I had to come in fully awake, to be fully prepared. I knew they would be waiting for me, with a myriad of possibilities to ambush and destroy. Two years previously, just around the turn of the millennium, I had tried to come in then, to '*walk into*', the bodymind of Chris Bourne.

We had a sacred agreement - our souls were matched by an allied yearning: it was his destiny to ascend and move on; it was mine to come here and confront, yet again, an Opposing Consciousness that I had been tracking and been tracked by for eons. We knew each other well. It was a cat and mouse game, but who was the cat and who the mouse? Sometimes it was hard to tell. Two years previously, it had resulted in Chris being forcibly detained in a German hospital, by those with no understanding of Kundalini Activation. He was pumped full of drugs, until the expanded consciousness of a rapid spiritual awakening, had quickly subsided - sunk once more, back into the darkened depths of hellish asleepness.

In 2002 we tried again, and once more they were waiting. This time they engineered a car crash, on a busy midday motorway, a flooding of the senses that made Chris question his own sense and sensibility. It should have resulted in a multi-car pile-up, but that was not the destiny of the day. A heart-felt upwelling, from the team I work with, initiated what I can only describe as a 'quantum phase shift': a collective yearning for justice, for rightness; a primal scream of such intensity, it shifted time and space. All the cars came to a halt, with not one smashing into the other. An impossibility in normal time space, but otherwise known as a miracle, in the place I call home.

It took quite some time for the switch to fully integrate. For several years, both our souls co-existed in the same bodily field. Sometimes, the soul of Chris was taking the lead; at other times, I was. And frequently, both souls were blended together. Yes, it was an incredible head spin! It all depended on what was to be learned, what was to be integrated. It was his destiny to bring into being the philosophy "Five Gateways", with which I assisted, by helping him through them experientially. I activated resonant inner feelings, to which he was able to attune and integrate. In return, I received an intense re-familiarisation with just what it means to be human.

He was exactly the right character for the mission I came here to accomplish: someone whose passions were stirred by the achievement of excellence; someone who had pushed himself to the limits physically, psychologically and emotionally. Forged in the crucible of high intensity sport, academia, business and the military, it was a bodymind that could carry the mission well. But first, I had to remember exactly what the mission was.

As a soul suddenly buried in the density of the physical, then subjected to the intense trials and tribulations of this plane, you quickly forget the place from which you incarnated. It disappears, literally in a flash. Even if you are still awake to your interconnectedness with the divine, your soul takes on the landscape into which it is incarnated. My home had, very suddenly, become a distant dream. I could recall the tunnel of light down which I descended. I could recall the formless space of infinite peace from which I'd come, but other than that, initially, there was very little else.

I needed to remember, but not just as thoughts and ideas. I needed to embody the fullness of my higher, cosmic self. And I needed to empathise with those I had come to help. I needed to experience the sense of lostness and disconnection, from their perspective. For only then, could I truly understand. I had to know what it was like to become a desensitised Homo Sapiens, and then unravel the path back to divinity, back to the divine being I could feel at the core of me. I had to journey back to Divinicus, and to share the experience with those who might hear.

The journey I am about to share, takes place mainly in the time period 2005 to 2013. The previous soul had essentially ascended, although was still lingering to a degree in my fourth density field. So I was still experiencing some of his filtering. At times, I felt like him, *the old Homo Sapiens*, but as these veils steadily fell, more and more, I was beginning to feel like the real me, like Divinicus. This then, is my journey, my story. It contains subjective perspectives of reality, which I am not claiming to be absolute truth. I believe in them passionately, or else I wouldn't share them. But all souls are subject to varying degrees of distortion, depending on how much the lens has been polished. No one is perfect. So my purpose is not to supplant your reality with mine. Rather, it is to catalyse a shift in consciousness, that a higher evolution of your own truth may unfold.

You may also find some of my views quite controversial. They frequently contradict those of the spiritual mainstream. It is my feeling, that many metaphysical beliefs have been allowed to settle as 'the truth', without a thorough exploration through the depths of the soul. So I encourage an open mind and heart in relation to the views I put forwards. I offer my perspective as a mirror to your own reality. What do you feel? What do you experience is truly going on in the multi-dimensional field all around you?

So as you read this text, I suggest you use it as a vehicle to challenge and expand your reality. Enjoy the experience, but pay close attention only to what resonates, for although it is my journey, it could well reflect a good deal of yours too.

from my heart to yours,

Open

PROLOGUE
Ghosts in the Machine

"They'll be waiting."
"Yes I know."
"It'll feel like dropping into a war zone."
"Yes I know."
"You'll likely forget your connection to us."
"It's happened before."
"No worries, we'll be there to remind you."
"In that I trust."
"You must become as a ghost in the machine"...

"I can feel him calling now, drawing me down."

"Yes it's time to leave. Farewell brother, see you on the other side."
"Farewell."

1

It all begins with the Oracle

"How else can you know something as real,
unless it rattles you to the very bones of who you are?"

The divine had quickly reconnected with me, and begun speaking through signs and synchronicity, an age-old mother tongue that captivated me to the core, pulling heart strings that frequently melted me to tears. This made more sense than any teacher, any book, any rhyme or reason. It was pure poetry, that resonated truth deep within. How else can you know something as real, unless it rattles you to the very bones of who you are?

I'd been taken to meet the 'Oracle', but I hasten to add, not the one of the iconic "Matrix" film trilogy. This was the Oracle Shopping Centre, although the signs and symbology you could find there, were no less compelling and poignant. I find the divine uses the full scope of possibility, in today's modern life, to reach out to us. This 'Oracle', was in the English city pronounced 'Redding', although spelt 'Reading'. *"Are you reading this?"*... the humour of divine guidance often cracks me up!

From the instant of my incarnation, I knew I was being watched, tracked by an 'Opposing Consciousness', using any method to get into my thoughts and emotions, to throw me off track. However, they couldn't accurately mimic my soul frequency, and the telepathy with which I was now being guided, sung like choirs of angels, into the very fabric of who I was.

A merry chase of heart-felt-pull, intertwined with consciousness 'spiking' (guiding an open mind with spiked, resonating synchronicity) led me around corners, up and down escalators, in and out of shops. Over many lifetimes I'd been taught this, thoroughly, with patience and great persistence: *when in this kind of density, where there are those that would try to control and deceive you, how even your thought-level consciousness can be read.* I was painstakingly reminded of how intention and desire can be perverted. Even to the extent that when you do something, it's easy to be duped, deceived into believing it's what you wanted to do all along. I'd been shown to master every base level desire, so that I could intimately know the authentic pull of my soul, in any given situation. The sheer intensity of it, often led me to feel like I'd been thrust into the plot of some Hollywood spy drama!

This merry chase led me first to HMV, where the angelic lyrics of the in-store music confirmed for me I was on the right track, correctly aligned with the flow. But the resonance inside told me this was not my final destination, not what the Oracle ultimately wanted to show me. You have to be so careful, not to get locked in the mind by the matrix's games, careful you're always connecting with true feeling.

The resonance had gone quiet now. I waited, and did the only thing that made sense in my newly incarnated being. I felt. And I felt. Felt deeper still. Because that's what being truly awake means: *to **always** come from deep inner feeling.*

A slight tingling kicked in, something I knew intimately: an energy, that was now moving and beginning to move me. It took me gently out of HMV and into the shop next door, Waterstones, the book store. The pull gathered and rose like a swelling tide, guiding me effortlessly around the first island of new releases, but then dumped me, very purposefully on the beach, in front of a cliffhanger of best sellers. *"Voilà, this is what you're here for,"* was the deep inner knowing.

"So what do you want to show me?" arose a soul initiated question.... *"Open your mind. Be still. Watch. Feel".* I knew the guidance as truth, so I intently surrendered to its wishes. My attention was guided, from book to book, in a seemingly haphazard way, connecting combinations of words that jumped off the covers to answer heart-felt questions. Realisations were landing left, right and centre. Tears welled up, the orchestra was playing a tune in my heart, just for me. But then something stopped me dead in my feeling tracks. A combination of book titles struck me, like a lightening bolt to the third eye…

"Homo Sapiens….a correctable mistake"

Wow! Something stirred deep within. Waves of energy began to surge through me; ancient memories filled with anguish and pain. But I couldn't go there right at that moment. I could feel the threads of consciousness now activating in my Akashic memory, but Waterstones was not the right place to unravel them. This story was going to take time and patience to fully unveil.

2

The Magnificence of Original Humanity

"There's total openness. The complete absence of fear.
There's an interconnectedness, both with the divine heavens above,
and also the physical 3D-world down below."

It was the next day now, early morning, 5am, meditation time in the darkened quietness, before the grey bearded beast breathes its morning fire into the matrix's energetic confusion. A consciousness spike draws me to the shower. I'm feeling the warm water rushing over my body. Senses are increasingly heightening now. I'd already moved to a vegan diet, so my vibration is quickly elevating - there is much less density to clog inner processing. Practically every hair on my neck is tingling.

I'm guided to switch from warm water to cold. There's a slight mental resistance, but the pull is unmistakable. My body initially retracts at the iciness, but I already know not to be governed by such reaction, rather to soften into the tightness, and attune to the truth of authentic soul-feeling through it... *because this is what the divine being in us does.*

The thread of inner vibration touches something deep and unmistakable. Suddenly, I'm propelled into a lucid dream. I can feel myself as an early human. I'm now feeling very primal. Something like Cro Magnon rings strongly. Days previously, I'd been guided to give up washing with soap. Now I understood why exactly. Without the distracting desensitisation of sterile, synthetic, sanitation, my sense of smell heightens sublimely. The authentic aroma of pure, muscle-pumping human, fills my nostrils. Unmistakable: natural pheromones - a 'body shop' the matrix is totally clueless at copying. "Why would anyone ever want to suppress something so original, so naked, so pure, so perfect?" *"A good question indeed"*... resonated the reply... *"Be patient, all will come".*

I'm now outside, walking through woods, following rabbit trails and the scent of other animals. There's an incredible flow of naturalness. Literally every leaf and stone is speaking to me, guiding me to a destination of rightness, sinking deeper and deeper into the essence of what I now am.

There's total openness. The complete absence of fear. There's an interconnectedness, both with the divine heavens above, and also the physical 3D-world down below. It's all a seamless orchestra of sound and synchronicity. The dawn song of a blue tit is speaking to me. Not that I have to interpret it with ever-so-clumsy words. It completely bypasses the intellect, connecting seamlessly with inner knowing. The blue tit sings, a heavenly shift happens inside, we are dancing together. This is true multi-dimensionality... *and this is the divine being within, which I'm sure you know as well.*

I don't want this to stop - to *never stop*. I'd give up absolutely every thread of anaesthetising desensitisation that the matrix has to offer: every gadget, every widget, every 'soft shoulder' to debilitate myself upon. I'd give it all up, for just another day of this interconnected perfection. If there was a God who designed this, then 'she' was a genius!

Suddenly, and inexplicably, like a creeping nightmare, my experience changed. It contracted, *down-graded*. Now I'm in fear. The blue tit continues to sing its merry tune, but all I want to do is hide behind the next obstacle, the next boulder. I'm terrified: afraid for my life, for my loved ones and off-spring. And I can feel something else now, coursing through my veins: something I always knew in the background of my Homo Sapiens experience. But just like the air, although coursing through my every waking moment, I still couldn't see it. Now though, it was like thick, black smoke, bellowing from some concrete power station. It darkened the air with density, like cheap perfume gone stale. Just one word... Control.

I could remember it well, from earlier in my existence. Control was the answer to this omnipresent fear. If I could control everything around me - my environment, my food and water supply, plants and animals, energy and resources, the people in my life - then I could be safe, my future ensured. Control had become my very reason for being, just like every non-awake human on our planet right now. It was the purpose that had gotten me through the day. Control gives meaning to the matrix. It makes it work, all cylinders rotating together, like the most over-designed car engine. Control is the common denominator, the language that gives sense to the matrix. And now, I was no longer the gracefully expanded and fearless Cro Magnon. I had instead, become something lesser, more confined, more enslaved, much more closed down. In a word, I had been *neutered*. I had become Homo Sapiens.

How did this happen? Why did it happen? Even with the depth of this re-familiarisation, that was, to me, more truthful than any sci-fi film, the fact that the answers to these questions were not immediately obvious, that pieces of the jigsaw were still missing, caused me to doubt. The fact that I couldn't immediately see the perpetrators and ask, *"Why did you do it? What on Earth could be so valuable as to cause you to do that to a human being?"* What on Earth, indeed. But all these answers would come; in time, everything would fall into place. And Benevolence constantly reminded me that the past was much less important than the future. That if I wanted to recover 'me' - *just as if you want to recover 'you'* - we have to focus. We have to feel any automated reactions to the moment - *any contractions* - and expand ourselves out again. And so, for some considerable time, for several years, this was my singular objective. First, I needed to remember the route-map back home; I needed to re-establish the Five Gateways.

3

Natural Selection, or Unnatural Intervention?

"Heaven knows, people might actually begin to discover who they truly are, where they've really come from, and, most importantly of all, where they're going to."

It was during the Fifth Gateway – *the Resurrection* – where I started to come fully into my being and the human story activated again. I knew that if I were ever to share it with the outside world, many would be understandably sceptical - humanity has been spoon fed the step-by-step, *natural evolution from the apes* story, since the time of Darwin. What I felt was necessary, was a way of challenging that widely accepted - *very conditioned* - view. Because as you begin to shift such entrenched consciousness, it makes the intellectual landscape, in which souls find themselves, more pliant and malleable. It softens the tightened inner world, so that a more expanded reality becomes possible. So what would help, is some physical evidence that humanity has been tampered with; evidence that might cause others to question the rigidly held science. So if I could find an exposed thread in the science and pull on it, then this intellect-based straightjacket, might just start to unravel. Minds might open, and then literally anything would be possible...

> *Heaven knows, people might actually begin to discover who they truly are, where they've really come from, and, most importantly of all, where they're going to.*

For me, the revelation of deep inner knowing, backed up by synchronicity, spoken in the mother tongue of the universe, is far more powerful than any intellect-based debate. That said, I do believe the spiritual view must directly relate to scientific evidence, otherwise it risks floating off into the realm of the surreal. For this reason, our spirituality must be very grounded too.

There was a knowing within me, that if humanity was engineered and down-graded *(as by now I knew to be the case)*, then the physical evidence had to be out there. It had to be somewhere in the fossil records. And I believe it is, for everyone to see, loud and clear. A spiking pull guided me to the internet, whereupon, *(through one of those wonderfully synchronistic dances across the keyboard)* I came across the work of a courageous soul called Lloyd Pye. It is so often the case, that no matter how withering the system is to the masses, a lone person will stand up, cross the parapet, and despite the boggy mud, razor wire fences and the metaphoric machine-gun fire with which they try to shoot you down, nevertheless, deliver a vital message with valiant courage.

As I read his book, "Intervention Theory", I knew instantly that there was truth in it. Yet again, it was one of those events that resonates deeply through you; one that sends shivers up your spine, making the hairs on your neck stand on end. The science can argue all it logically likes, but it matters not a jot, when you can truly feel something in the depths of your soul.

In summarising the main resonance in his work, I could point to the fact that of all creatures on the planet, Sapiens is supposedly the most highly evolved, yet with the most genetic coding errors by far. We have several thousand, compared to the odd hundred for the average animal. Or I could point to the 223 genes - the building blocks - that appear nowhere else in any other life form, except in the Sapiens body chemistry. I could point to the fact that there simply hasn't been enough time, for the changes necessary, to naturally evolve a great ape into a great human. I could point to the missing link, which is still missing. I could ask why our bones are so much lighter, more brittle and, pound for pound, why our muscles are half as strong. What possible evolutionary advantage is that? And as I read, with 'pennies dropping' line by line, it occurred to me, that if you took away centrally heated homes, tools, energy, clothes and agriculture - *because none of these are natural to any other naturally evolved creature* - how many of us would survive a few days or even a week? Go out into the streets. Take an objective look at how Sapiens lives. Open your mind for a moment, and contemplate the stark staring obvious:

> *we are the most evolved creature on the planet, yet without the iron lung the matrix provides, we are by far the least adapted to living on Earth – at least as nature designed it. Take away all of the things Sapiens has come to depend upon in society, unplug the life support for a moment, and many wouldn't even make it through a few cold nights.*

It struck me how amazing it is that Sapiens is so incompatible with the natural order of life on this planet; so challenged is he by the natural eco-systems that thrive here. He is so unnatural, and yet, *has 97% the same DNA as a chimpanzee.* No wonder the Darwinians assumed a straight evolutionary unfolding from apes to humans. And I agree, the Sapiens past must have quite a degree of common ancestry with the apes. However, one hurdle to the straightforward, path of natural selection, stands blatantly – *like a sore thumb* - in the way. This hurdle is carefully concealed at the heart of our cells, and although microscopic, the truth it reveals is immense - *Earth shatteringly immense.* What I'm speaking of, has the power not just to challenge the traditional science, *but to unravel it.* This ticking-time-bomb for the natural selection story, is carefully concealed within our chromosomes.

As I continued to read Lloyd's book, a metaphor of the 'tree of life' sprang to mind: *if genes represent the leaves of the metaphoric tree of human life, then chromosomes are the twigs that the leaves hang upon.* Each cell within Homo Sapiens has 46 chromosomes, *23 matching pairs of twigs,* one half from the mother, the other half from the father. All great apes and hominids, from which we're supposed to have naturally evolved, have 48 chromosomes; yet we have only 46. Traditional Science explains this curiosity with the fairly flippant answer, that the 2nd and 3rd chromosomes in each of the paternal and maternal lineages must have become fused at some point during our 'ascent' from the apes. And indeed, under a microscope, it's clear that these chromosomes have been fused. But how? *"Spontaneous mutation"* - the evolutionists strongly insist, as they push this unwelcome truth gingerly back under the evolutionary rug.

So I began to contemplate deeply, the likelihood of this lynch pin in the Darwinian story. My thinking went something like this: All humans have 46 chromosomes. In all of us, the 2nd and 3rd chromosomes are fused together, both in the paternal and maternal lineages. Yet here's the crunch, that hit me as hard as a hammer:

> **this chromosome fusing is not what makes Sapiens human, and offers no natural evolutionary advantage, yet all humans have the mutation. How is that possible?**

My journey through the plane of the intellect quickened. For the natural selection story to be true, it would mean that, somewhere in Sapiens ancestry - *in some missing hominid link* - the mutation would have to have occurred spontaneously, in the egg cells of one of their off-spring. It's further complicated by the fact that this 'shift' is not just one mutation, but two: the 2nd and 3rd chromosomes are fused in both the paternal and maternal lineages. Assuming they didn't happen simultaneously - *because that wouldn't be step-by-step natural selection* - then the Sapiens genome must have passed through a stage where all humans had 47 chromosomes - *that is for the mainstream view to hold water.* Yet we don't see a history of successful humans with 47 chromosomes, only the double mutation of 46 that we see today.

And because you don't find any Homo Sapiens with 48 chromosomes, then somehow, this very curious, very rare, and very complex mutation sequence, would never-the-less, *had to have succeeded, even though it offers no natural evolutionary advantage.*

Quite the contrary - in fact, the mutation is a natural evolutionary **disadvantage**: for successful breeding to happen at all, the chromosomes of two breeding parents must 'line up'. Although sexual reproduction would not have been impossible between a '48er' and '46er', it's been clearly shown, that when successful, such hybridisation tends to lead to miscarriages, genetic disorders and infertility; in a similar way to Down's syndrome for example.

In other words:

the fitness for survival would have been extremely low.

Maybe then, some unnatural hybridisation - *some intervention* - is one of the key reasons why humanity is so highly evolved and yet is so unhealthy with so many genetic disorders? Disorders - such as infertility - that would seem to be strongly on the increase. It occurred to me (and surely it must to you too) that this is not the measure of a successful and natural evolution.

However, because it's so prominent in the mainstream theory - *so embedded within our conditioning* - let's consider the natural selection possibility of this 'spontaneous mutation' (of the chromosomes) a while longer. At the outset, once you had a creature with the mutated 46 chromosomes (which seems completely unnatural in itself), there would have been only a 50:50 chance for the mutation to be passed onto the offspring - half would express the 48er configuration, likewise the 46er. And considering the 48er would have been the most genetically aligned and strong, over time, the likelihood is that the 46er mutation would have been mostly bred out. It begs the extremely inconvenient question:

so where are all the modern humans with 48 chromosomes?

For the mainstream natural selection view to be true, *all modern humans must have descended with 46 chromosomes from one original being, despite being the weaker configuration.* Unless that is, they're arguing that the mutations happened in one breeding male, **and** one breeding female, **in the same location and time** - then the mutation would propagate. But think about it for a moment, the odds of this happening, are so incredibly low, as to make it practically impossible: two identical mutations, *(that in themselves are extremely rare and difficult)* happening in the same place and time, to one male and female egg, that then safely grew to maturity (in very unsafe times); that just happened to meet, reproduce and *give birth to the entire human race.* How likely is that?

But here's the other crunch, the other flat-liner to the natural selection lifeline: for the mainstream view to be true, because you get no modern humans with 48 chromosomes, **all others from the stock species must have then, by some 'natural means' died out, despite having the strongest genetic stock.** And in case you'd somehow forgotten:

> **the chromosome mutation is not what makes Sapiens human and offers no natural evolutionary advantage whatsoever - in fact, it is an evolutionary disadvantage.**

For the stronger species to just mysteriously vanish, is not natural evolution - it's not natural selection. You could argue perhaps (as some mainstream scientists do), that during some cataclysmic global event, the evolving humans were thinned down to a small group - *miraculously the group with this very unlikely mutation.* And you could even argue that the dominant alpha male *(who just happened to be the one with the mutation)* impregnated *all* the breeding females in this one, very 'blessed' tribe. Of course the odds are thinning all the time. But even if theses events were remotely possible, this **very fortunate alpha male with 46 chromosomes, would still have fathered offspring with 48.**

This very inconvenient truth, doesn't even end here. There are nine other - *seemingly insurmountable* - hurdles for the evolutionists to conquer. In nine other chromosomes, there's been what's termed an 'inversion'. As I understand it, our chromosome 'twig' on the tree of life, has a top, a middle and a bottom. An inversion is where the middle, for some particular reason, *breaks apart, rotates through 180 degrees and reconnects again.* Curious. Very curious. The evolutionists argue once more, that this happened by spontaneous mutation. But the argument still doesn't escape the fact that there's no natural evolutionary advantage - *they're a reproductive hurdle.* Why is it then, that all humans - **all Sapiens** - have not just a few, but **all nine of these identical inversions?** For the natural selection model to still hold any kind of water, these inversions had to happen sequentially - one at a time. And with each progressive inversion, there's still the 50:50 chance that the previous chromosome configuration (without the mutation) would thrive - especially since it's genetically more aligned. Yet there are no Homo Sapiens **without all nine inversions.** How, by natural selection, is that possible?

So let me spell out what is now – *surely* – entirely obvious: it is practically a mathematical certainty, that **Homo Sapiens did not evolve - by natural selection - from the apes!** The great ape genetics must have been used as the foundation stock for our species, yes, but for these ten 'mutations' to have happened at all, they had to be **engineered that way.** Yes, let me say it again, so that the energy and reality of it can land fully home:

> **for these ten 'mutations' to have happened at all,**
> **they had to be engineered that way.**

There's no other viable explanation. These chromosome changes were **engineered.** And as this realisation dawned deeply in my awareness, it also, practically simultaneously, initiated the very obvious question... **"Engineered by whom, how, and why?"**

4

The Engineering of Homo Sapiens

"Why did they do it?"

In my continued explorations, although something was already itching under the surface of my skin, and even though patience was not one of my strong points, I was clearly told I'd get to the 'whom' and the 'how' later. Suffice it to say, it was immediately obvious that whoever did it, must have been highly evolved, with tremendous insight into DNA manipulation. They must have had highly advanced technology to do it... *"experienced engineers yes, but not necessarily highly evolved,"* was the instant reply to my chain of thought. Although to the uninitiated, it may at first seem the work of a deity, as my fingers journeyed the web, it became abundantly clear you don't have to be a god to master such engineering. Quite recently in fact, Russian scientists have claimed to be able to change the egg of a frog, into the egg of a salamander, simply by projecting laser light at it. And in spiritual circles, we're proving that even carefully spoken words, *of the right frequency*, can alter a person's DNA. So you don't have to be a god to do it. You just need the will, a degree of knowledge, and some technological sophistication. *We can leave the question of integrity until later!*

I quickly realised there are actually not one, but two parts to the question... *'Why did this engineering take place?'* There's the basic, scientific question of why the chromosome changes were engineered – especially if it generates no natural evolutionary advantage. And there's the more complex, philosophical question... *'Why would these (fairly) advanced beings embark on such an Earth-shattering Intervention anyway?'*

I felt to deal with the basic question first: *'Why engineer the chromosomes?*' So I investigated the chromosome number more deeply. But rather than dash around the keyboard haphazardly, I sat quietly in meditation, opened up to those who had reconnected from the higher dimensions, and were thus far guiding me so well. It didn't take long *(for the divine being in us, it never does)*. The image of a horse lit up in my mind. Although it wasn't a full blown, muscular power-house, as they usually are. This one was smaller, like a mule of some kind. So that's what I looked up next on the web. What I discovered led to another one of those deep *'aha'* moments of knowing. The humble mule has indeed an interesting chromosome story to tell.

I discovered that a mule has 63 chromosomes. It is the cross-breed of a donkey with only 62 and a horse with 64. *But the really interesting point, is that all mules are infertile.* Mules cannot bear offspring. While they may indeed mate, the only way to reproduce a baby mule is to cross-breed once more a donkey with a horse. This seemed deeply poignant. So what might that mean for the chromosome story of Sapiens?

Then it dawned on me. Imagine yourself as an advanced, extra-terrestrial, inter-dimensional being for one moment. Let's suppose you had - *what was for you* - a 'good' reason to manipulate, shape and engineer the genetics of another species on this planet. Clearly, the agenda involved inserting some of your own DNA – hence the 223 genes that appear nowhere else in the Earth's tree of life. And you'd certainly want to use a stock species that was well adapted to life on the planet, one that was intelligent, one that might have the wherewithal to fulfil your agenda. So you'd choose something like the great ape - *a hominid* - which had become highly evolved, adapted and intelligent. Hence the fact that we have 97% the DNA of a chimpanzee.

However, having made the DNA changes to create your new species, the last thing you'd want to happen, is for it to interbreed with the old stock. Why? Because if you'd introduced new genetics that fulfilled your agenda, *especially if those changes weakened the original stock*, then the likelihood that cross-breeding would eventually dissolve out the new genetics is quite high. Especially if the new species' bone and muscle strengths were a fraction of the original design. That's when it dawned: here's why they made those chromosome changes...

When a species with a particular chromosome configuration, tries to breed with a related one that is different, the chances of producing successful offspring are radically reduced. It can be sufficient to create barriers between different species lineages.

That's why **all** Homo Sapiens have only 46 chromosomes and none have 48. They wanted to make sure their DNA changes weren't bred out naturally. To me, it was the only possible reason that made any sense. The ten so called 'mutations' of which the evolutionists speak, have no other earthly advantage, rhyme nor reason. Homo Sapiens was purposefully engineered, full stop. There's no other reasonable possibility. And I put it to all reading, it's time we got to grips with it, because it has far reaching ramifications. It begs the much more important questions...

By whom? And why did they do it?

It could not have been straightforward. So why did they go to all that trouble? What might have compelled them? The answer wasn't immediately obvious. And it also occurred to me... *why the necessity for the nine inversions?* Because splicing the second and third chromosomes together would amply suffice. The reply was immediate..."*Be patient, all will come!*"

5

Benevolent Guiding Presence

"A true master has reached the point of evolution where 'he' knows that 'he' is an eternal student."

I was crouched on bare earth, huddled in a confined, seemingly primordial place, shoulder to shoulder with a dozen or so sweaty, naked and nervous human beings. It was pitch black. The branched roof of the construction - an arched dome, formed from bent over saplings covered with blankets - forced my back uncomfortably forwards, tucking my head down, as if sitting in a foetal position. If there was any way of being more uncomfortable, I couldn't at the time imagine it.

This was my first Sweat Lodge. It's an ancient shamanic practice that rebirths you from the womb of Mother Earth, and as I was soon to discover, can abruptly reconnect you with the heavens above. It's dark, close, confined. It can be terrifyingly shattering, yet spiritually nurturing, all at the same time. As glowing, red-hot rocks, roasted for several hours on an open fire, are served into the central pit, a primordial smoke fills your nostrils, burns the back of your throat, fires your heart and pumps your lungs.

To the uninitiated, a Sweat Lodge can be hell **and** heaven, both at the same time. And that's exactly how I experienced my first one. I was ready. I'd travelled a good way. I'd surrendered a great deal. Now was the time to truly push the barrier, to see where it might take me, what might I remember? Not that I was trying, not that my mind was efforting, I could simply feel the upwelling of readiness through every cell of my being. It was time to enter the crucible. Time to be 'reactivated'.

Some people are physically able to suppress the intensity of the experience, but I wasn't in a place to want to do that. I'd opened up too much to close down now. Whatever came, was going to seep mercilessly into every pore of me. And so it did. Like a fire breathing dragon, the intense heat swallowed me whole, and within a short space of time, I was sweating profusely, my heart beating as if it would explode, my lungs were pumping madly, to redistribute excruciating internal tension. I felt like a rocket on a launch pad, all engines scorching fuel, ready for lift off.

Then boom! Suddenly I'm way up in the cosmos, two places at once. In the higher, I was in a formless place of absolute perfection and clarity. In the lower, it was like being crucified in the raging fires of hell. It was as though I was simultaneously dying **and** in heaven. How curious! It wasn't until later, that I realised it was because *there were still two souls in Chris' bodymind field*. Somehow, the intense heat and karma of the experience temporarily separated us.

Whilst all hell was breaking loose down in the Sweat Lodge, up in the higher dimensions, suddenly 'they' appeared, as if from nowhere. I did not see them. I could not see anything, for there was simply no form to be seen. This was pure white light - an infinite ocean of consciousness. Although I couldn't see them, I knew them well. It felt as if they were woven through every fibre and cell of me.

They spoke, but not in words. Words would be too clumsy for this level of evolution. The only way I could describe the communication was as '*telepathic knowing exchange*'. They resonated a vibration, and like a warm blanket, enfolded me in it. This loving embrace activated a resonant frequency within me. It wasn't that anything was transferred as such - *there was no channelling*. For them, that would be too invasive, too influential. It was more that they offered me the opportunity to be open, activating something that **already** existed within...

This was my first encounter with what I've come to know as "The Group of Nine". And since then, because they've always extended an open hand of benevolent friendship, I now call them more simply, "Openhand".

This was the 'Team' that had been so expertly guiding me and reacquainting me with the Human Intervention story. And they're there for you too, should you feel the resonance to connect. But just as with me, they won't tell you your truth. They certainly won't spoon-feed you. Because that risks being too influential, too overriding of your own perspective and free will. Instead, by working through the weave of the patterning of life, they offer a point of view. If you open your heart to them, they'll shape synchronicity around you, thereby presenting a mirror, asking you the question...

"This is what you're being now, does that serve you?"

As I came to realise, they'll never tell you your truth. But they'll work tirelessly to help you discover it for yourself.

Steadily, I began to remember them. Many a time my heart was melted by the simplest synchronicity, seemingly crafted just for my own eyes. I recall an amusing exchange in a spiritual seminar. The leader was a very accomplished, international spiritual teacher. He was speaking of synchronicity, and at one point, poked some harmless but meaningful fun at the 'New Agies'... *'You know these New Agies will be seeing signs and synchronicity everywhere. They'll try to create meaning where there is none. A leaf floats by your window and it has some profoundly important message.'* To which, a cackle of laughter broke out in the group. But at that exact same moment, my attention was spiked, my awareness drawn outside the room, *as a leaf floated down past the window.* 'Whose having the last laugh now?' I couldn't help smiling to myself. And within, I could feel the Team laughing with me, through me. *I'm sure you've had similar - these are the priceless experiences that can so light up our divine lives.*

The Team are etheric, formless, highly evolved. They are what many call "The Ascended Masters". Yet I hasten to add, they would accept no such term for themselves… *"There is always something to be mastered, therefore the term 'master' is a misnomer. A true master has reached the point of evolution where 'he' knows that 'he' is an eternal student"* (please note: as I share some of the exchanges, although depicted in conversational form for ease and clarity, it was always through assisted self-realisation - *beyond words* - that we communicated).

Why nine? "Because there are seven rays of consciousness that form the known, experienced universe. Therefore seven of the Nine are the 'tillers' of each ray. They help ensure its free, uninterrupted flow through materiality. They activate and vibrate resonant frequencies, as the consciousness gets blocked in eddy currents, somewhere down the universal line. Number 8 harnesses the natural harmony of the group, so the Nine can manifest somewhere, and 'speak' as one. As for number Nine, she relates the incarnated experience back to the Group, and 'steers the correct course' - so to speak. We act separately, and yet together as one. There are also two others outside the group, like the number 10 for example. She's from the angelic realms, from a parallel universe, holding the wisdom from the previous experience, and so is profoundly trusted to help direct attention to wherever it needs to go. And we'll come to number 11 later.

What is your purpose?… "We're working to bring the known universe to nirvana - balanced harmony between unity awareness and separation awareness, in every part of it - so that all sentient life can co-exist in peace. Thus each can experience the fullness and beauty of the soul beyond limitation, yet without transgressing or harming the integrity of other sentient life."

How will you achieve this?... "We trust that it is the natural
harmony of life to reach this state of perfection. We don't
seek to change the outcome of the individual journey of any
sentient form. We respect the universal right of free will. We
seek, therefore, not to over-influence. Like a catalyst in a
chemical reaction, we don't change the course of the reaction
itself, rather we help bring it more speedily to its inevitable
conclusion. We work by presenting a mirror, resonating
frequencies that reflect how someone is being: both the light
and darkened sides. By providing such a mirror, buttons
are pushed, light activated, and that sentient life-form is
empowered to evolve. But it is always **their** choice."

Since my initial encounter, I've travelled through the realms
many times with the Openhand Team. I have seen many visions,
which helped integrate and explain why things are how they are
on Planet Earth right now, and exactly why humanity is suffering
as he is. It was this divine connection, that helped me understand
why the Intervention happened here in the first place.

During a sleepless yet restful night, relaxed and softening ever
deeper into the expansive experience of soul, I was lifted up by
the energy of the Team, through the dimensions, into the Akashic
Record and projected right back to the formation of the universe.
There, I was shown how three, quintessentially important, "Original
Mistakes" (*there's no such thing as a mistake unless you fail to learn
from it!*), shaped the Intervention humanity is now experiencing.
This is what was shown and 'described' to me (remembering it's all
about assisted self-realisation)...

*At the singularity you have Pure Presence. The One. The
Absolute. It's that which still exists, throughout the manifested
universe, in and through all things. You can know it in the
background of experience. It's that which precedes your
experience. When you're in Pure Presence, and still flowing
with the experience, it's what's called an 'enlightened state'.*

Back at the beginning, immediately prior to what humanity

calls the 'Big Bang', Presence had subdivided into two flows of consciousness: separation consciousness flowing outwards, and unity consciousness flowing back inwards (I liken it to the undertow on a pond). As the waves of separation consciousness multiplied, a chain reaction caused the Big Bang; as the waves rippled outwards, their wavelength increased and thus their frequency lowered. They got denser and the pull of unity consciousness back to the Source caused them to condense into form. In this way, the eleven dimensions - more accurately described as"densities" - took shape. Within those, the further subdivision of separation consciousness and corresponding impulsion of unity consciousness, accelerated evolution into what you have in this moment - the entire cosmos teeming with life.

Now at some point in this dynamic, self-awareness happened. In other words, awareness of the One Self - Pure Presence (I sensed this caused some great degree of excitement!). And there came with it, what can best be described as, a 'reading of the flow': an observing and sensing of where the flow was going. But at that point, it hadn't yet been realised, that the observer and the observed interrelate. Thus you effect what you observe. As the One began to predict where the flow was going, it 'froze' reality, creating a snapshot in time (like taking a photograph). Temporarily the One became lost in the form, eddy currents shaped around what was being observed, which then shaped new manifestations. The more that is being read, the stronger the focus, and so what you're ultimately left with, is a consciousness that controls realities. Thus the first Original Mistake was formed: that of "Controlling Reality".

The One continued to self-realise through the ever flowing, ever changing, and sub-dividing universe. Over time, it got ever closer to knowing itself as an experience. But there came a point, when it realised it can never truly have an experience of itself as pure, unadulterated presence, because experience can only be had through relativity of form. Therefore, although you can get very close, you can't experience presence as a relativistic experience. Although you can realise it as a 'non-experience'. It is the sense of emptiness and everythingness through all things.

At this point, you might say 'sadness' happened. It occurred because of the noise of the universe now created; the realisation that although you could know Pure Presence in the background of experience (tasted as a non-experience), you couldn't ever experience that through the manifested universe. The relativity of form creates the 'noise' of separation. What's more, you couldn't do anything to switch it off! This sadness caused another eddy current to form in the flow, and with that, other manifestations of density. It's the second Original Mistake, which we may call... "The Pain of Existence".

At some point afterwards, the One unravelled itself from this distortion (what I'm calling a 'mistake') and let itself be free to experience the ever-manifesting, ever-shaping universe, without limitation; with what was then experienced as joy and pleasure. But with that, it began to lose itself ever more within the creation, becoming increasingly invested in what was forming. And thus the third Original Mistake happened..."Revelling in Physicality".

Once such a distortion in the flow of reality happens, then eddy currents of manifestation form within the separation consciousness, into which unity consciousness is drawn. As souls evolve - each being a flowing experience of the One - they are drawn into the density of the distortions, to play them out, unravel them, and find realisation of the One Self once more. So this is the beginning of the cycle of karma and reincarnation - karma being the energy that is built due to the lower self-realisation; in other words, identification with the form in some way, draws an unrealised soul into it.

What this means, is that all manner of chaos, confusion and control has been created, in a myriad of different forms, which some souls 'willingly' take on (there's no real choice!), in order to resolve out. That of course includes the Intervention that has so controlled the Earth and humanity upon it. It's a process playing itself out right across the universe.

This was absolutely amazing to me. Now I remembered, as a deep inner knowing, why it had all taken place, and why exactly I was being chased around by some pretty unsavoury, inter-dimensional characters. Although any form of judgment was already beginning to fall away. It also helped make sense of an earlier experience, a short while after my incarnation...

an experience with the 'fallen angel'.

6

The Fallen Angel

"Where there's a genuine yearning for growth, understanding and evolution, the universe works tirelessly to provide you a mirror. And I would say: especially accept the mirror where it is unpleasant."

Chris had separated from his wife and two children shortly after the car crash. His awakening - *and my incarnation* - was so earth shattering, that it instantly shifted his consciousness into a new way of being. It brought him into frequent confrontation with the matrix, due to the illusionary self and reality he'd created. As I'm sure many of you will have discovered on the path, sometimes those realities can bend, evolve and find new harmonies. Sometimes however, they have to break.

Chris had gone to live locally, within easy access of his children. In their formative years, clearly it was important they had plenty of continued interaction, love and support from their father. But even though he loved them dearly, he still knew it was the right choice to be separated. Who can say what the karma for another person is? Is it right to deprive someone of the destined path they came here to live? Even if that involves a degree of challenge, pain and suffering? And so it became obvious to Chris, that it was more damaging to stay, where the disharmonious environment evoked constant energetic tension. It was right to leave, but also right to be supportive, from a distance.

So Chris stayed close, yet in the breathing room of his own expanding inner space. Day by day, his sensitivity to universal life-energy intensified. Working from the farm where he lived, afforded him immense opportunity to connect with the land, the trees, the natural wild life; to awaken every day to the poetic dawn chorus.

More and more, this deepening connection to universal awareness was activating the divine light within. He was passionately committed to making the most of it. As for me, I was now mostly supporting from his fourth density field.

It was about this time, that he began to have his first, direct experiences of the Intervention. And it was also a powerful time of re-education for me. Most people are unsuspecting: they simply don't notice the shadows of Opposing Consciousness that lurk in the fourth dimensional web-matrix; that which so influences their lives. The drama of daily life is so full of distraction, that most people's attention is constantly focused externally. It's either struggling in some way to survive, or else easing the pain through some kind of 'entertainment'. As I quickly came to realise, it's not humanity's fault, it seemed society had been purposefully created to achieve this: *to distract people from their inner world.* Since the experience we have is mostly created by where our attention is directed, most miss the inter-dimensional interplay going on within their own being. They've been closed down and shut off to it. Neither is the problem solved by simply expanding into the higher dimensions through meditation. Only by penetrating the density of the inner layers, can the Intervention first be fully seen, and then, fully ejected.

Yes, we are multi-dimensional and, most importantly, we are **influenced** through multiple dimensions: *even if people are not always aware of it.* Well, Chris became intently aware one evening, as he went to visit his children, to read them their bed-time story. I share below from his memoirs...

By now, I was super sensitive, and when I entered the house - a typical middle-class, executive ladder-climber - it was like walking into a thick blanket of energetic smog. I could feel the appliances and the electricity buzzing in the walls. The 'cleaning' chemicals seemed to seep into every pore. There was a TV soap opera vibration that hung in the air like stale cigarette smoke. It seemed to infuse the very fabric of the brickwork.

This is how I had lived. It was quite shocking.

However, not as shocking as what was about to take place. It was merely the warm-up routine. Something else would emerge from the shadows to steal the limelight. It began with my son, who appeared first - tense, wound-up, in quite a tantrum. But then he disappeared into another room, only for my daughter to appear. There was no usual hug and angelic smile this time; instead, just like my son, anger, tension and frustration. She disappeared only for my son to reappear, now calm, smiling and connected. What on Earth was going on? Then it was my wife's turn. She appeared, spitting fire, whilst my children had apparently both morphed into heavenly cherubim. Deeply perplexed, I marvelled at this interchanging drama, where a very definite energy seemed to move sequentially from host to host. Wow! What an eye opener.

It wasn't until a couple of days later, that the full significance dawned in Chris' awareness. The 'pull' drew him into the local video store to a Denzel Washington film called, very appropriately, "Fallen". It's quite a disturbing film, about a serial killer who is brought to justice and put to death, only to have his demonised soul live on in the surrounding field; passing from host to host, possessing people and living its life by aggravating their inner energy. At least that's the multi-dimensional metaphor you can take from the film.

To me, it made absolute sense, the reactivation of something I'd known so well. A heavenly interaction with the Nine confirmed it: *Yes, there are entities living in the field all around you. Yes, they do possess and invade people's bodily fields. Yes, they've created the matrix of mass human subconsciousness, in which the planet is entrapped, in order to enslave and extract energy. As Morpheus so accurately said in the iconic film, "The Matrix", 'it's to turn a human being into a living battery.'*

Although I could feel the confirmation of my own inner truth, at the time, it was still pretty hard to digest and sit comfortably with. I knew I would need more close encounters for the veils to fully fall; that I may understand and accept the presence of this Opposing Consciousness. And I would say to anyone reading, who's sceptical about this phenomenon, yes, it's right to be that way, until you experience it for yourself. But do explore. It's abundantly clear to many in the world now, that humanity's natural state of multi-dimensionality has been contracted down. The inner layers have become so compacted and dense, most can't feel the subtle interplays that are influencing them. But where there's a genuine yearning for growth, understanding and evolution, the universe works tirelessly to provide you a mirror. And I would say: *especially accept the mirror where it is unpleasant.* I have discovered, time and again, that this is where most is to be gained.

It was this approach that helped me quickly penetrate the illusion of the darker side of the inner world; so vital to my re-education. I recall staying at the house of a spiritual friend, in a quiet suburb, in the heart of southern England's upwardly mobile, London commuter belt. It was not the kind of place you'd immediately associate with an encounter with Lucifer: *the bringer of light through the exploration of darkness.* But then, who was it who said our ignorance and bleary eyed denial is the greatest evil of all?

I awoke in the middle of the night. It seemed I was fully awake, although I later reasoned that I must have been in a lucid dream-like state. It was a multi-dimensional experience, but within physicality. It was one of those occasions where, in one moment, you're zoned out, gone with the wind, and in the next, eyes wide open. You're instantly present: *here, now, stomach already nauseating with some, as yet, veiled anticipation.*

It began with a cold tingling, that iced its way up my spine to meet the rising hairs in the nape of my neck. It was immediately followed by an undeniable pull: *"Get out of bed,"* was the quiet but insistent inner voice, *"there's someone for you to meet - a part of your education."* So I eased my way out of bed, legs like jelly, as I made my way precariously to the door. I so wanted to turn on the light, but it was quickly clear, that this experience was meant to be had in darkness: *perhaps so I could more readily empathise with the being that had lurked for eons in life's blackened recesses.*

The pull was drawing me downstairs, and with each creaking step, the tingling up my spine and the twisting nausea in my stomach, ratcheted up another notch. As I descended the staircase, it became suddenly colder, and by the time I reached the door of the living room, at the end of the downstairs corridor, my hands were shaking. There was a foul stench seeping under the door, and a deepening sense of foreboding at what might await inside.

The last thing I wanted to do was enter the room. But the soul in me already had the upper hand in life. Enough of 'me' had surrendered to the learning, remembering, evolving purpose of existence. When the soul approaches a crossroads with one direction pointing to hell, and the other to heaven, the choice is made purely by the opportunity for growth and expansion. Anyone can shine their light when it's sunny. Besides, you have to keep reminding yourself this is all just a transient experience; not who you are - which is the inviolable "One".

Although I could still feel the presence of Chris within me understandably resisting, in this dream-like state, I was in the driving seat. And so bit by bit, creak by creak, I made my way gingerly into the room. The lights were out, but a lucid, multi-dimensional movie now began to roll: *in the middle of the room was a Beast. There's no other way to describe it. Seated on the floor, it filled the space all the way to the ceiling with its grossness. Its blackness exuded a stench, that made me so want to vomit.*

Helplessly, I was drawn ever closer... *it's all just an experience!* I could see its blood-red eyes, yet it looked not towards me. It was only when I was right up close, that its pulsating head turned slowly to encounter mine. As its piercing eyes stared downwards into my very soul, I was ready to retract, but for a dialogue that opened between us - not one of words, but telepathy:

"*Who are you?*" asked the Beast. I didn't have to think for the answer, it just seemed to pop up... "*I am the light.*" "*Yes you are,*" came the knowing in return, "*Let me tell you about me: whereas you were the light, a 'chosen one', to experience heavenly Ascension, I became your opposite. You cannot have any experience without relativity: 'this' in relation to 'that'. And you cannot truly express your light, until you have cleared all the inner darkness veiling it. Thus, to know yourself as unconditional love, you must manifest something that would cause you to hate, that you may let go of such judgment. Hence it was my role to descend, draw and manifest the density of God's distortions - the 'mistakes' of existence. I am the one 'cast out of heaven', fallen into the abyss, holding a universe of denseness, so that souls like you can rediscover and experience their light. I am the 'fallen angel'.*"

This struck home in the centre of my heart. Yes indeed, it was my own judgment of 'black' and 'white', 'right' and 'wrong', that had created the distorted form of Lucifer - *this beast* - sitting before me now. If you want to be a candle in the darkness, you have to create the darkness through which to experience it. Immediately, my feelings began to soften. And with that, the floodgates of realisation broke wide open. The judgment in my heart dissolved, and in its place, I found acceptance...

> I could be the One by integrating any sense of 'right' and 'wrong', by dissolving such judgment. Yet at the same time, I could have the relativistic experience I was now experiencing.

Now the tables turned. As I looked into the eyes of the beast, I could only feel respect and compassion. My self-righteousness softened into a sense of warming openness. As the veils between us fell away, I could taste (as my own) the eons of abandonment and isolation this soul had felt. And I remembered that there is only one Self; each soul being a stream of consciousness from the One. So this 'beast' is actually an expression of me (and you too!). Despite knowing what this 'beast' - this soul - had been labelled with, I simply wanted to embrace it with love.

Although this actor in the drama of life had experienced being divorced from the 'love of God' for an eternity, it still recognised love in my eyes. With that, it could no longer contract downwards in hate and loathing. It softened and eased, before suddenly exploding into flashes of coloured light; penetrating out through the walls, and perhaps into every darkened recess of the universe. Lucifer could not hold the tightness of the fearful veil a second longer. Such is the power of unconditional love. Wow!

And so this was my introduction to Lucifer, in this incarnation. Some while later, after I'd travelled yet further down the path of re-acquaintance, I would be ready for another encounter: *to fully understand the direct role, in the human story, of this magnificent and selfless angel.*

For now, it was time to experience other distorted manifestations of 'God' in this realm. Remembering that, by the Law of Attraction, we, as souls, only ever manifest reflections by which to see ourselves more clearly. If we're unconscious anywhere inside, if we (as a soul) become disconnected from the Source that we are (if we become divorced from 'God'), then these 'blind spots' are going to be filled by 'shadows'; inter-dimensional entities can move in and possess our vacant inner world. There they remain, manifesting disharmony in our outer lives, fractionating true alignment, until we go within and reclaim our focus; until we reclaim our sovereignty.

The time had come to get to know this 'Opposing Consciousness' more intimately.

7

Buckle your Seatbelt, Dorothy!

"The Isle of Avalon: to those who are sensitive, arriving here is like stepping into a portal of multi-dimensionality - another world - and the Tor is its stairway to heaven."

My journey led next to Glastonbury: *the heart centre of our planet.* I'd picked up my very psychically gifted friend, Tanmayo, from Heathrow Airport, someone I'd met a while back down the path. She was one of those wonderful starsouls, who seem to drift into your life from some distant galaxy. Wherever it was, she was certainly not of this Earth, with a reading of the flow and the inter-dimensionality of life that you seldom experience in another human. Her frequent international travels, meant that unfortunately, our meetings were rare, but when they happened, they were simply electric: gripping the edge of your seat kind of stuff - the kind of experiences that good movies are made of. And so it was, as we departed Heathrow, I looked across into her eyes, winked, and spoke the immortal words...

"Buckle your seatbelt, Dorothy,
'cos Kansas is going bye bye!"

Little did I know, that it was a part of me that would be leaving.

We were on a magical mystery tour, simply following the pull, my favourite game of 'free wheeling'. You just ask the question: *"Where would you have me go now?"* then wait for some kind of feeling or knowing to land. Tanmayo immediately got the sense it was either Glastonbury or Totnes, both highly energetic and spiritual locations. Having been to neither, I knew I was in for a treat. Although I held the space for both possibilities, nothing landed until the very last possible junction: *"This way or that?" Glastonbury it was!*

The Glastonbury Tor is an amazing sight. Rising majestically up through the perennial mists of the Somerset levels, you can see her from miles around. With her citadel-like tower right on the peak, it's like walking into a scene from "Lord of the Rings". You can imagine how, in ancient times, she drew the faithful from far and wide; *such is her majesty.* For no coincidental reason, is this place called by locals, "The Isle of Avalon". To those who are sensitive, arriving here is like stepping into a portal of multi-dimensionality - *another world* - and the Tor is its stairway to heaven.

Although still several miles away, my first sight struck a deep chord within. It reminded me of another sacred site, Mow Cop, in Cheshire, middle England. As the similarity struck me, I could strongly feel the resonance of Chris, who I knew had a profound connection to Mow Cop. Chris was the reincarnation of, amongst others, Hugh Bourne, a famous pastor who'd had a profound awakening and connection to the Christ Consciousness. He'd become a Methodist preacher, and so resonant were the words which emanated from him, that even in the 19th Century, long before the internet and telephone, he drew thousands of spiritual seekers from far and wide. And it was at Mow Cop, bearing very similar hallmarks to the Glastonbury Tor, that his clan gathered.

Suddenly it dawned on me: *I had a picture of Hugh in my car boot!* The frame had been broken somehow, and I was intending to take it to the repairers. It was a picture drawn by a psychic artist, who'd looked into the eyes of Chris and seen Hugh. As I recounted my 'coincidence' to Tanmayo, she smiled knowingly... *"So what do you feel to do with him now?"* The question instantly took me deep within. Knowing was landing, and a welling up of tears signalled this was something deeply significant for me: *"I should ascend the Tor, up through the mists of Avalon, with the picture of Hugh/Chris, and ceremoniously release his soul from my body."*

And so I did. Ascending the Tor, I noticed its seven incremental layers, representing the seven main chakras. And I could clearly feel the spiralling movement of energy around it, through what I would later discover, is its concealed labyrinth. Such is the mysticism of this magnificent megalith. As I rose through the layers, I could feel the soul of Chris, readying to leave. I laid his (Hugh's) picture down carefully at the sixth level, and made my way emotionally up to St Michael's Tower, standing majestically on the peak, at the centre of the seventh layer.

Inside the Tower that day, I felt and experienced many things: I felt the presence of Lady Avalon, as if the Tor was her curvaceous body; I felt the soul of Chris, separating from mine; The Group of Nine were there, helping bring greater sensibility; and all were held in the cradling arms of Gaia. *What a remarkable place this is!* There was a deep sense of home-coming, arriving back into the heart of me. It was then that my soul name first came to me in this incarnation - "Open". A spontaneous ceremony of deep feeling took place in the tower; the feeling of being 'baptised' - recognised for who I now was.

However, it wasn't all rosy that day. There was another vibration present, one that I'd all-too-easily overlooked in the swirling majesty of the ceremony. Unknowingly, an unconscious inner blind spot had allowed in a frequency that didn't belong. In the days that followed, the flow seemed to strengthen greatly. It was what I'd expected. I knew that when you embody soul so strongly, it could literally move mountains. And so the path seemed to effortlessly open up for me... *"Perhaps this is what it really means to be 'Open'?"* I can clearly remember thinking. Everything seemed to click into place. I'd be driving into a city, and all the traffic lights would turn green, just as I approached them. This was amazing!

However, something didn't sit right with me. There was the niggling question of doubt in what I was experiencing... *"How can it be that everything effortlessly manifests for me, without the slightest consideration for anything or anyone else?"* This was the thought - *the unconsciousness* - that I kept pushing down, unwilling to fully accept... *"This must be the feeling of God, it's surely right that I should be able to shape the world around me."* Slowly but surely, the experience began to unravel: *"the flow must consider all life, not just mine."* It was then that I felt it for the first time - a spinning vortex above my crown, that felt like the chakra, but instead of bringing soul fully in, it seemed to be spiralling it out. This was my first experience with energetic implants, carefully concealed within our unconscious blind spots.

It angered me. I'd been deceived. But I still wasn't sure exactly how. All I knew, was that the usual creative vibration of manifestation now flowing through me, was tainted. Another, more subtle frequency was feeding in with the flow. What could I do? I took myself up to the Tor, and from a high place, 'prayed' for help. At that moment, the powerful tenor Pavarotti began to sing "Nessun Dorma" in my mind. Any sense of anger now hackled the warrior in me instead: I let go of the need to spiritually manifest; I let go of needing to do anything; I even let go of my new name, lest it had become some form of spiritual identity. Instead, I brought my consciousness deep within my body, down into the base - *the power bearing dantien* - and yelled a primal scream, that echoed through every cell of my being.

The spinning vortex was unceremoniously ejected from my crown, and a beam of intense, fourth density light, projected out from my third eye, which instantly obliterated the source of the implant and its connected entity. Upon which, began a psychic attack of such intensity, I thought I might die. The energy that had come in on my soul vibration, that had tried to befriend me, promising all manner of metaphoric 'riches and jewels', recognising that it could no longer fool me, turned in on me, and launched a full-on assault. I remember it well, like the scene from "Batman", as the terrified young child is swarmed by angry, biting, bats. But Benevolence was with me too: *"It's only energy, it's only a transient experience. Become as nothing in it - become the One - until your enemy has nowhere to strike."*

And so I softened, and penetrated deep within the feeling of it, became as one with the biting pain: the hazy confusion, the sense of disconnection. This is where my unconsciousness had allowed in the Intervention. The pain itself, was where the path of light now needed to go. Releasing the need to spiritually manifest in any way, I allowed myself to become fully human. Although there was the palpable sense of being spiritually disempowered, it felt very real, very grounded, very here. At which point, the attack ended. They were wasting their energy - I'd become completely internally congruent and aligned. Thus they couldn't 'see' me anymore. To them, I'd become a ghost in the machine.

I soon came to realise, this dimming of the higher spiritual power, did, in no way, mean disempowerment. As we all must come to terms with at some point, I just had to get used to a new kind of density and lower frequencies of feeling. In so doing, I discovered something crucial: *fully grounding soul into the depths of the physical, was by far the best way of defeating the Intervention.* You had to be fully grounded in feeling, **as well** as being centred, aligned, and connected into the higher paradigm. It was the implant - *a twisted coil of energy* - that had surreptitiously prevented full soul embodiment, and with that, created a veil through which the Opposing Consciousness energies could invade my being. In the years that followed, I'd discover more of these, both in myself and in many others too.

It became clear, that these implants are a key feature of the Intervention and downgraded experience of Homo Sapiens. Everyone has them. They work by resonating a distractive frequency of vibration, that draws attention from a key soul centre. It then becomes as 'white noise', which you start to ignore, as it slips silently into your psyche. Now 'someone' else is pulling the strings within you; you're unwittingly releasing emotional energy into the field, which is their source of 'food'. It means they can see you, just like a heat trace on a thermal imager at night time. In this way, the Opposing Consciousness is farming humanity, just like people farm sheep, pigs and cattle: *a karmic mirror that mankind would do well to digest.*

Some while later, as I'd begun to guide spiritual work, I experienced the dehumanising impact on other people too. There were twelve of us, sitting in circle. I'd already guided several days helping people confront inner blind spots and dissolve them away. With minimal external distraction, the group's inner sensitivity was heightening. Apart from the sound of nature - the cleansing rush of a nearby stream, and the odd chirping bird - it was intensely quiet. All nervous fidgeting - caused by unwinding minds, detoxing from society's busyness - had long since dissipated.

Suddenly, apparitions appeared in the studio. Not everyone could see them - your inner eye has to be highly active. But probably, all would have felt the change in energy. These visitors looked like so-called "Ascended Masters". The room filled with a rosy hue, a blissful energy, which began to melt away the pain of human existence, elevating you into dizzy heights of blissful connection. Wow. Most were blown away by it. Literally. Souls we're reaching up into this blissful state, stepping out of the pain of incarnation - the density of a bodymind. It's like eating your favourite sugar-coated chocolate bar: the taste softening you, releasing endorphins, that oh-so-feel-good-factor, for a while. But then you become addicted, and the vibration of what you've consumed corrupts your authentic signal, so that you can't quite feel it anymore. The real you is buried in it.

Sitting next to me was my newly rediscovered soulmate, Trinity, a highly sensitive empath, with a deep connection into the angelic realms. She knew exactly what was happening, and telepathically brought my attention to the problem. The entities had been drawn in through the karmic connection with a member of the group. It wasn't that person's fault of course, unwittingly it happens to many. What transpired next, was that Trinity willfully insisted these so-called Ascended Masters move on. The energy was dispatched, the rosy hue dissipated; everyone came 'back to Earth' once more. The point is: that you can unravel *through* the bodymind and thereby transcend it. This is the true path of spiritual evolution, not distancing oneself in denial, as is so often the case these days.

What's needed now, is that clearly contesting consciousness, to discern the truth from the lie.

In time, I would remember: we become sensitive to these implants *(and their attached entities)*, only when we stop allowing ourselves to be distracted from the place of authentic manifestation - *the Source itself*. And this can only happen by becoming truly selfless. If we're seduced into the need for some kind of external outcome, then attention shifts into the outer mirror, instead of being secured in the Source of true creation. But when there's the commitment to divinely aligned service, attention can surrender fully into the depths of our being. And with an open mind, *one that's prepared to challenge all 'sacred cows' and all spiritual identities*, you'll begin to know when something feels right and when it's distorted. You don't have to effort, it's like falling in love. And when a truth of beingness lands for you, then you have the power to remove the implant from your field. You have to feel it, get the sense of how it was put in; and, by surrendered will, eject it. It takes skill and sensitivity, yes, but where there's a will, there's a way.

In time, I would also come to realise that these entities and their implants, as unpleasant as they are, actually serve an invaluable purpose: *they create the mirror of unconsciousness that we must work through*. It was a realisation that would serve me well, as I came to see the full magnitude of the deception that humanity had been enslaved within. And I would offer it to you too, as a valuable means of penetrating the inner world, if you can do so without judgment and anger. It's a realisation that can help you greatly.

For now, at this point in my journey, removing the crown implant and thereby being able to come deeper into my being, meant that I could feel much more of the surrounding energy field: I could gain ever deeper insight into the human story (I'll share more on implants later in the journey). Crucially, it means that as you begin to remove these implants - *the spiking sources of 'heat'* - the entities see you less and less. There are fewer unconscious blind spots - you become that 'ghost in the machine'. And what's more, the heart-felt pull strengthens, you become more accurately guided in life. It's like having your own personal 'Messiah', inside yourself!

8

The Messiah Within

"Every moment reveals an aspect of truth about yourself to yourself, and there is absolutely nothing else going on."

It was around 5pm, Friday evening, at my new home with Trinity in Glastonbury. It was the end of January 2006, and the rent was due promptly on Monday morning. The trouble was, we didn't have a bean to bless ourselves with, let alone the mountainous £700 cost of the rent. I'm sure you can empathise: even if you've not been there, it's one of those classic situations that can make the Sapiens in you squirm, in this world of deadlines and debt. What could we do? I had to rediscover what walking the spiritual path truly meant: *how a heart-felt pull can guide you, and just what authentic manifestation is really all about.* To do it, I'd need to call on the Christ Consciousness and, who knows, *maybe even JC himself!*

Most people in society are so closed down, so inwardly suppressed, that tightness to the world's broken promises, dreams and expectations gets inwardly compacted, like layers of silt at the bottom of a meandering stream. But when we let the light in, it stirs up the sediment, and reclaims the lost nuggets of soul gold, that have long been buried there. Each internal confrontation will come with a degree of challenge and pain, as the sediment activates and washes away. But the reintegration of those lost aspects of you, becomes totally sublime. I'm sure you've been there: waves of relief, remembrance and joy, remind you of that home-coming feeling; a familiar, accepting and totally natural sense of you. I ask you...*what could be better?*

As I'd discovered earlier on the path, in order to truly experience this as a way of life, a threshold has to be crossed - *there has to be complete surrender to the divine.* And for this to happen, a fundamental realisation has to be made (see below). It is not one we can simply make with the mind. We may get a whiff of what 'walking the spiritual path' means beforehand. But to truly 'get it', we have to dive headlong into the raging torrent of life, with abandon, so that it literally takes your breath away.

As I sat wondering how to pay the rent, I was remembering this fundamental realisation: that whatever objectives, desires, ambitions or dreams we may have in the outer world, these are merely the effects of internal consciousness; they are merely mirrors to our inner self. If we spend our lives trying purposefully to shape the external world, according to some mind-led agenda, then the expectation will always fall short of the universe's authentic purpose for us. Or, worse still, our efforting might pull in the unwanted attention of Opposing Consciousness. A close connection with the Team affirmed it for me...

There is but one purpose to every moment. Irrespective of what temporary objective you may be utterly engrossed in, there is always one underlying reason: everything is connected by threads of consciousness, One Self, seeking to experience itself through every soul. Each is a piece of a universal mosaic, and every moment configures perfectly around the purpose of self-realisation. Creation is there to reveal an aspect of truth: about yourself, to yourself. And there is absolutely nothing else going on. Ever!

As this remembrance settled once more, it turned the life into which I had incarnated, literally on its head, so I could shake out any remaining cobwebs. It meant I could approach each moment in a new way. There was no longer winning or losing. There was no right or wrong. 'Black' and 'white' had merged into the grey areas of life - *the blind spots* - for which I now had to take responsibility. Abandoning the intense inner inquiry of the moment, to a system of ideas, beliefs and blindfolded conditioning, would no longer suffice. It was time, once more, to own the awesome sovereignty, of the *constant conscious choice.*

This creative creature in the heart of all people, is what I've come to respect, admire and cherish as the "Christ Consciousness" - our own personal Messiah. It can light the grey areas of our inner world, illuminating the choices that need to be made. It is to move beyond judgment, for judgment only ever ties us to the old reality, just as outward-projected-blame only ever holds us down. By the Law of Attraction, we've drawn to ourselves every facet of our lives - the good, the bad and the ugly. This is so we can keep making those judgments, until we realise they no longer serve. And the only way to move through, is to accept the life we create. The outer drama, no matter how challenging, we manifested because of our own inner darkness. So we must look into the mirror, observe ourselves honestly in the cold light of day, then figure out what judgement of life might have created the current experience we're having.

And I'd say: we also need to expand our understanding of what 'judgment' really means. It's not just about blaming or adversely criticising someone else. It's also when we hold some kind of limiting opinion about life itself. It's an internally fixed relationship to reality, around which we inadvertently create attached dramas - eddy currents of the Original Mistakes previously shared. So for example: *"I've got an old injury in my neck which is an incredible pain (the Pain of Existence). If I exercise, it's just going to make it worse, so I'd better not."* And so the injury is semi-permanently cemented in our consciousness, and therefore limits our experience by a fixed opinion of it. It's just another example of an unconscious blind spot forming.

As I was carefully lowering myself into incarnation, I was experiencing both the joy and the pain, knowing I had to allow myself to experience the full depth of feeling: the immense joy of interconnectivity, but then feeling the suffering of another, as if it is your own. The sweet and the sour, often come hand in hand. By giving yourself intimately into every experience, without forming some limiting opinion of it, then you can feel more not less. You're never restricted from life's fullness. When we can accept both the pleasure and the pain, without ownership or rejection, that's when we're beginning to taste the real juice of life. It's another key signal that we're evolving from Sapiens to Divinicus, and activation of the Christ Consciousness helps us do it.

The Christ Consciousness ignites in the heart when we can be totally accepting of the moment. And synchronistically, at this point, I started encountering people following the Christian path. It soon illuminated for me the perverse paradox of the Christian religion: *"I am the way, the truth and the light, no one comes to the father but through me."* I cannot believe, for one moment, that any being as evolved as Jesus - one truly carrying the Christ Consciousness - would have said that. For in itself, it is a gross judgment, not only of the path, *which has been rendered as a singular way,* but of anyone else not walking a Christian path. Which, in itself, is just not, well, Christian!

I pondered if somehow it was a mistranslation? And then a synchronous 'chance' encounter, yielded another interpretation:

*'I am' **IS** the way to the truth and the light.*
No one comes to the father but through the 'I am'.

Now this I found interesting, because it would bring Christianity right into line with Buddhism, for example *(and no doubt countless other religions and spiritual practices).* What it surely means is to look into the outer world and embrace the 'I am' within it - *'I am that which I have created.'* It is only by such acceptance of reality, that you can slowly but surely, bit by bit, lose the sense of separation from all; lose the judgment that creates the small 'I'. Thus we drop into the Void of non-identification, the place of infinite potential, the sense of presence that is the 'father' of all authentic experience. It was clear to me, that non-judgment must be the only way to become the 'father' - *to truly become the One.*

Neither does non-judgment mean the wishy washy acceptance of 'anything goes'. It has to be so much more than an intellectual idea of letting go. I came to observe, frequently in spiritual circles, that some groups advocate 'dropping the hot coals' - but before they ever truly allowed themselves to feel the heat of the moment. So you become that which is attached to non-attachment. It's like a fail-safe trip switch has been installed internally: *"Oh that feels hot, that's uncomfortable, better drop those hot coals instantly, so everything feels cool again."* I'd realised through my own previous 'mistakes', that this is not the way to true non-attachment. It leads, instead, to a life of denial.

I recall my very first firewalk: I'd been directed to focus intently on the far side and walk purposefully across the glowing red coals; I'd heard in other practices, you focus the mind on something like wet moss, *for this is about mind over matter.* What a disappointment! All that emotive, soul-stirring build up, and it was over in a flash - I hardly felt a thing. I resolved that the second time would be different: *the jembe softened me deeply into the rhythm of the moment, my body gently rocking, a dance that guided me slowly out into the middle of the coals. Breath drew the intense heat of the fire-deva up into my body, cleansing and burning away that which didn't belong. And there, right in the middle of those burning red jewels, as I worked to transcend any inner retraction, a young shaman came to me from a reservation in Taos, New Mexico. I'd witnessed him earlier that year, performing a Native American corn dance. A bond had formed between us: "nothing to fear brother, dance with me and drink in the juice of life!"*

This is what the so called 'non-dualists' out there are missing. It's another 'mistake' - *a misunderstanding of the eastern teachings* - which I started to encounter quite frequently. The Void of the Absolute - *and the divine experience that flows from it* - can only be experienced by softening into the full flavour of the moment. There can only ever be an experience at all, if there is relativity, if there is still the sense of 'this' and 'that'. So what I often see going on, is a quasi-denial of the relativity, and in so doing, dropping into an isolated bubble of non-attachment: *of intellectual Enlightenment.*

It's dropping the hot-coals just as soon as there's a prickle of heat. Thus, they don't truly feel the soul and the magical path of light that unfolds from it. You can only do this when you keep dropping truly into the Void of emptiness – of infinite potential. And since the Void is to be found in and through all things, you can only experience it by surrendering completely **into** *all experience: you have to feel, not just the early prickle, but the blazing heat of the moment so that you become totally one with it.* Then you simply fall into the Void, through the heat, and authentic experience arises from it. All of this was quickly falling back into my awareness, as my own resurrection unfolded. I knew it was the Christ Consciousness - *the Messiah within* - that can help unravel attachment, and align us with the natural flow - *through this 'crucifixion' of life's materiality.*

And so it was, as I'd eased myself back into the fiery heat of life, it left me one Friday evening at my new home in Glastonbury, unable to pay the rent: *now see how easily you get owned by those beads of sweat, as they trickle down your forehead!* Yes I could feel the inner contraction, that earlier down the path, would have been experienced as fear and flapping. But now, instead, I knew to feel the vestiges of fear and soften into it, to feel through it. And if I truly did this, I'd open into the Void of infinite potential again; whereupon, something would arise – *an expression of authentic beingness* - that would light the way.

What I came to experience, time and again, is that if I surrendered to this natural directional impulse of life, then the universe would always provide me a 'vehicle' through which to express (*I'm using 'vehicle' here, in the widest possible sense of the word*). There will always be some event, circumstance or experience, that would enable you to express an aspect of truth about yourself. What's more, such authentically aligned expression would **always** be resourced by the universe in some way. There would **always** be the fuel for it. I think Paulo Coelho, in his wonderful book 'The Alchemist', phrased it: *"when you follow your heart, the universe works for you"*. Based on countless experiences, I totally concur.

So I was sitting at the kitchen table, feeling the last vestiges of fear and using breath to help soften into it... *"follow the thread of consciousness and the universe will always find you a vehicle through which to express."* Bingo! Why not sell my car? It was a bit of a button pusher: in this realm of density, a car, after all, does provide a sense of freedom... *"freedom is a feeling you have inside."* Yes indeed! Of course I know that. So I let go of the physical need for freedom, upon which, I found myself expanding blissfully inside...

> *You see, this is the point: what's going on in every moment of life, is a co-creative flow, that at a higher level, you've already subscribed to. And the purpose is what? Yes... "to reveal an aspect of truth about yourself to yourself." So you've already subscribed to a higher learning vehicle, with others; which is some kind of abstract contemplation of the nature of reality. Within the new Divinicus design, there will be a flow of this energy, that interacts with your etheric bodily vehicles, to shape the external reality around you. In fact, Divinicus or not,* **you already are** *shaping your reality, just with the blockages and resistant eddy currents built in. As you are inside, so you manifest into the outer world.*

This particular 'vehicle' of higher realisation, was the exploration of divine trust: of non-judgmental discernment; and also, the true nature of resource. This last one, for me, was particularly poignant. Often we may think we have no money to do 'this' or 'that', and yet we still own resources. As I steadily transitioned from my old life filled with material possessions, the stuff I didn't need was traded for 'energy' that I did. The Team affirmed it for me: *if you own something, then you have resources, you have energy, which can be 'transmuted' into some other form.* In this case, I needed money!

So I decided to sell the car. I say 'decide', but a choice didn't need to be made. It simply became obvious: *committing to the path of self realisation means the choices simply make themselves. A path of light effortlessly unfolds before you.* So the question landed, *"how best shall I sell the car?"* As I'd already encountered in this dense place, the mind wants to answer such questions quickly. As Sapiens, we've been conditioned in society to having to produce some instant answer. Being wishy washy is not something that gets rewarded in the matrix!

As with many people, the bodymind I came into, has a powerful, logical, and very active lower mind - it can be quite a slippery snake, frequently wanting to own the show. So my abstract higher contemplation, about the nature of resource, trusting the flow, and manifesting a 'vehicle' of expression, instantly became: *"Let's sell the car on the internet, where millions will see it."* This was the logical thing to do. It would offer the best opportunity of selling the car quickly, recognising that the rent was due in only three days.

First though, was the unglamorous side: I needed to wash the car, which nevertheless, I did with enthusiasm *(after all, I was in the flow, the divine was creating with me)*. Next, was taking the photograph. Angling the lens and playing with the settings, the perfect shot presented itself, except just at that moment, a dark cloud passed overhead. I'd have to wait and try again. As the sky cleared, and I clicked the shot once more, once again, I was thwarted: *the batteries ran out!* Now normally in society, we don't read any deeper significance to the flow of such events. The Sapiens in us would simply head off to the nearest store, where there are bound to be more batteries; especially in a world which has been configured purposefully for instant consumeristic gratification. I came to realise: *this is what Sapiens is designed for - it's what he's meant to do.*

However, resisting any temptation to close down and accept some lower-life compromise, I could feel instead, the clearly recognisable, higher educational pattern of deeper significance beginning to kick in. I wasn't supposed to photograph the car. The synchronicity was obvious, even if the reason and next possibility were not. How did that feel? Together with a degree of nervousness, it simply felt right. So I asked the question: *"What would you have me do now?"* And the feeling was unequivocal - I should get in the car and drive.

Again, Divinicus always has to watch for when the mind of Sapiens wants to take the driving wheel and own the ride. Remember: *trust is the key to this healing process.* So I'm driving down the road, and my mind is already figuring out what it thinks I'm supposed to be doing next: *"Yes, you're meant to be going to your usual parking place, that's obviously the direction in which you're heading."* I'm sure you recognise this in yourself, at least sometimes - the mind adding two and two but getting five. Except this time, unusually, there was nothing free at my usual parking place... *"That's strange,"* I found myself thinking. Deeper significance was surely at play.

Once again, I needed to open the internal space, around which the lower mind always wants to contract, with some overriding and premature solution. When we do this, the spontaneous knowing of higher mind can effortlessly kick back in... *It has to be effortless, otherwise like soft, open petals at dusk time, it simply closes down.*

This simple 'knowing' guided me to take the next left. Driving up an incline, a car pulled out in front of me, making a sudden u-turn in the middle of the road. My attention was drawn to the number plate, with JC as the last two letters. There was a very clear feeling to follow the car. I laughed to myself... *"If JC wants to help me sell my car, well then I'm open!"* Despite the joke, I was clearly receiving a powerful remembrance of the Christ Consciousness, and how to work with it: *how to keep opening into the heart; holding back the contractions of lower mind; and feeling one's divine destiny.*

So I followed JC back down the road, next right, past my house and then left into Glastonbury High Street. The heart-felt pull was unequivocal. And as I'm driving down the High Street, suddenly a car pulls out with its hazard lights blinking. It swerved between me and JC. Somehow, I just knew the parking space it vacated was for me. So without hesitation I pulled in. *"What next"* I thought?... *"Easy. Park up, and put a price on it."*

It certainly wasn't the solution lower mind was comfortable with. After all, this was Glastonbury High Street: a small town, where most people have not too much money, and you don't sell cars effortlessly in just a couple of days. Still, the guidance was unequivocal, and yet again, I found the will to hold back the instant assumptions and conclusions of the Sapiens mind. I found some paper, a pencil, and wrote down my phone number, together with the price of £700 – what I'd paid for the car a year earlier, *and synchronistically what I now needed for the rent.* I simply knew I was in the flow - these 'coincidences' don't happen by chance. Now, feeling optimistic, I stuck the 'For Sale' sign in the windscreen and walked back home.

I didn't have to wait long for a response. The very next morning, around 9am, I got a phone call... *"I've seen your car for sale. Can I come over and chat about it?"* "Sure! Come right over, we're at No.9 just around the corner." A few minutes later, a knock at the door announced his arrival. As the door swung open and our eyes connected, it was one of those 'aha' moments, like déjà vu. Each of us was able to look with total transparency, past the eyes, and deep into the soul. It was self evident: *we had encountered each other in a past life.* There was that unmistakable, deep sense of heart-felt connection. I could hear the pennies dropping, even as we began to speak... *It's never about selling cars or any other kind of outcome. It's always about how are you being now? What's your highest expression of beingness? How easily might your soul be sold, because you're focussed on some expected or needed outcome?*

So an intense dialogue ensued for the next two hours. Many deep revelations and sharings took place. It was clearly one of those 'sacred contracts' that people speak of in spiritual circles: a destined exchange, designed to help each to unfurl something important. For me, it was all about watching subtle eagerness for lower mind to own the show; an ever-so-slight contracting down, believing that all parts of the puzzle had landed before they truly had. I was able to engage, but soften into this exposed contraction - a subtle one that I could clearly feel inside *(It's these blind spots that allow in the Intervention of Opposing Consciousness in some way. In this case: over-energising the logic function of the Sapiens mind).*

Then, just as that constriction had unwound itself, the conversation came to an abrupt and synchronistic end *(as if I needed the reminder that the inner shapes the outer perfectly).* We looked at each other for just a moment, which seemed to expand to eternity. Two souls had formed a mutually supporting feedback loop, that carried us experientially all the way back to the Source. Then suddenly, and in harmony, we both expressed together: *"What about the car!"* We laughed at the merry dance the divine had taken us upon.

What happened next was priceless. Precious. A sheer blessing. He reached inside his jacket, pulled out an envelope and slapped £700 down on the kitchen table… *"I'll take the car,"* he confidently announced. *"But don't you want to test drive it and check it out?"* I inquired. *"No need, I trust you."* Amazing. Awesome. Tears welled up. Of course: we'd connected across time, travelled through life and death experiences together. The car had been a vehicle for our joint sense of deepening and integration. It seemed right that we exchange. There was no need to deliberate. We could both simply feel it. 'This is divine manifestation at its purest,' I thought. 'Why can't it always be like this?'... *'It can. As long as you keep lower mind open long enough, for the soul to flow through, to generate its mutually creative feedback loops, then miracles like this will simply happen all the time. Try and stop them!'*

As the guy was leaving with the keys and registration document, I had one final question: *"What caused you to see the car in the first place?"* I was fascinated at the heavenly play of the divine. *"Oh yes, I was camping at a site the other side of the Tor. I'm feeling to live in Glastonbury. Your car was parked right outside the first estate agent I came to - And, I also needed a car!"* When two or more people are reading from such a 'divine script' – *the natural ordering flow* – then you get poetry in motion. It was an experience I would never forget, one that would carry me well, along the winding road ahead. Not to mention, I could now pay the rent!

So it was the inquisitive interplay of the Divinicus higher mind, that had facilitated this (almost) incredible sequence of events; followed by an activation of the 'Christ Consciousness', as a heart-felt pull. This often comes with the unravelling of any kind of fixed opinion about the moment, any kind of contraction, and too early focussing by the untrusting Sapiens mind.

What has this to do with the spiritual craze of 'envisioning', 'intentioning' and 'manifesting' the things you want?... *Zip. Zero. Zilch. Nada. Nothing! Yes, you may create something that way, because all is consciousness and connected by focussing threads; but it'll be an illusionary construct, a false reality, that'll surely leave you floundering in some side-tracked eddy current.* Of course, it's ultimately fear-based – not trusting in the natural flow of life. I wonder, what could be better than the kind of miraculous flow I've described in my story? What do you feel when everything is guided for you and clicks magically into place like this? For me, there's simply nothing to compare. It's priceless: *as if the whole universe is coming into alignment, just for you.* Surely this is the true meaning of abundance? And all you really have to do, is open your heart and let it flow in.

To me, this was the real lesson of Jesus, who I believe embodied the Christ Consciousness admirably. Throughout his life, he demonstrated the utmost importance of making the higher choice, at whatever personal cost. Even to his crucifixion, Jesus wore his heart on his sleeve, saying: *'This is the way to divinity. This is the way to Divinicus.'* I thanked him profusely for his re-acquaintance in this dense physical plane. In the journey that was drawing me ever deeper, the Messiah within, would prove utterly essential, in many a tight spot to follow.

9

The Truth Will Set You Free

"What's happening on Earth, is a full scale invasion;
a war on the very consciousness of humanity,
to which the majority are pretty much oblivious."

The lady was sitting on the sofa in front of me. By now, people were just showing up to see me, drawn I guess, by the catalytic consciousness that could activate their repressed pain and peel it away - *like past life karma.* She'd been feeling suicidal - not at all normal for her - but after a generally happy, and so far fulfilled life, she was finding it ever more difficult to be comfortable in her own skin. This is the fascinating thing about karma: it's energetic and fourth dimensional, yes, but its effects mirror through the physical body, such that the pain *is felt as physical.* And it influences the emotional and mental state too. All people have it, because it's what brought them here; they just don't know about it, until it begins to kick in.

  Suddenly, the lady went into spasms, her body contracting, face contorting. She was now lying straight, but struggling to move, giving the impression that she was somehow being restrained, held down, as if she was strapped to the couch. Now I began to see 'visions', some images yes, but more importantly, 'knowings' were landing about exactly what was going on. I'd opened empathic connections between us in multiple dimensions of reality. I saw that she was in some kind of 'operating theatre', but not of this world. It was a higher, fourth dimensional vibration. And standing around her, were the shimmering shapes of beings - *they had black, almond-shaped eyes.* I knew these, I'd seen them before. There was an instant sense of unease, which made my stomach churn.

It was clear she'd been abducted - *her vibration temporarily raised up into the Fourth Density* - a 'trick' these entities had become skilled at. What happened next was simply gut wrenching - there's no other way to describe it. With great care not to unduly influence the lady, I asked her what she was now experiencing. She was finding it hard to speak, and when she did, she spoke only a kind of gobbledegook. Then it suddenly clicked - *it was an alien language*. And at that moment, I watched aghast, with fourth dimensional eyes, as her entire body began to shake, decompose, and *break down into some kind of scaly slime. It was abundantly clear: she'd experienced DNA manipulation.*

By now, in this physical realm, as she relived the experience, it looked like the lady was going into shock. My energy changed, there was a sense of urgency - how to help? Then it came to me: *she has to feel this, she has to relive it. In that way, she can truly be released from the unconscious impact of it on her life. But she has to know this is just an experience, and she is not that; rather, she's the inviolable Source beyond it. I had to help her walk the blade edge of the experience - in it, but not lost in it.*

And so the words just materialised from my mouth... *"Don't worry, this is only energy, only an experience and it doesn't define who you are. All experience is merely transitory. Find the key that helps you unlock the doorway through the experience."* Upon which, she began to soften. Over the course of the next ten minutes or so, the pain began to visibly ease. It was clear - I simply knew - that in the regressed experience, after the horror, she had died. It came to me to ask her how it felt to pass on? She was now speaking English again... *"Release, freedom, lifting from my body, floating into the light."* I could see angels present, in the higher vibrations around us. And 'here', in the physical plane (on the sofa), her whole demeanour relaxed and opened, becoming blissful even. She was healing, the karma had gone, she would now feel comfortable in her own skin.

With increasing regularity, more and more experiences like this began to happen. It was a rapid refresher in the meaning of karma, and how to work with it. I could see it's a much misunderstood phenomenon here: *you don't store 'good' or 'bad' karma based on how you behave*. What's happening, is that the soul gets attached to past life trauma - how we passed on for example. So, notionally speaking, a 'fragment' of the soul 'breaks off', gets stuck in the experience, and therefore pulls in energy around it - like building swirling eddy currents in the stream, which drag in debris. This then gets stored in the causal body, in the Fourth Density. This is what causes our next incarnation, because the soul is yearning to be self-realised *through that experience*. In other words: *to be liberated from it*. It's how we evolve and grow. So no matter how challenging these regressions can be, they are the path to realisation, evolution and Ascension. I consoled myself (as I do others I now work with), that the beauty of it is, you don't actually have to relive the experience again in a physical way *(and that's the crucial importance of humanity now processing its karma)*.

I recall another experience, this time whilst facilitating a group meditation in movement. This particular lady assured me beforehand, *"I never have spiritual experiences!"* Yet just five minutes in, she came over to me with a very worried look... *"My head is disconnected, and it's over there on the floor, in the corner!"* By now, I was becoming pretty au fait with these kinds of occurrences, but yes, you have to find a steely nerve to deal with them. The point is: always to soften yourself, expand and allow the guidance of Benevolence to know what to do. In this case... *"Let's go over and pick up the head shall we?"* She agreed, so we recovered the head, *put it back on her body*, and then *I smoothed out her energy field with my hands*. She recalled afterwards, that she'd seen images of being beheaded in a past life. The fascinating thing was, that all her life, she'd suffered from chronic nerve pain, which no amount of traditional medicine nor treatment could cure. Now, in just a few minutes, that pain had completely disappeared!

It dawned on me, that the lives of many people are governed by fear of pain, and ultimately, by fear of death. So much of society is geared around taking away, placating or easing this pain. It happens either through comfort eating, soft drugs such as alcohol, external distraction, or some form of 'entertainment'; essentially 'popping a pill'. When in actual fact, *the pain is our path to freedom*. It's our reaction to the pain - *be it emotional, physical or mental* - that causes identification with it, and therefore defines us by it. But distancing yourself in denial doesn't help either - *dropping the hot coals before you've felt the heat*. That just creates the identity of avoidance. It takes true confrontation of the pain, becoming as one with it, to ultimately cure it. You must get to know the pain, *as if you are that*. Then there's no separation from it. In which case, *you can open the door through it*, and so rediscover yourself as the inviolable presence that you are... *"the One"*.

Death is just like this. In society, I came to see that there is a pathological fear of death. It occurred to me, that it's been created that way; inculcated by the Intervention into human psychology. You see the judgments of it in so many TV soap operas - *"how awful that so and so lost his life"*. You can imagine how much misery this creates. For most, this fear of death causes fear of life - the result is, that most hardly live at all. I reflected on Chris' car crash, which led to my incarnation. Perhaps, it was because he'd already faced death a number of times, that he was able to let go. Perhaps, he was just ready. Whatever it was, the letting go caused a complete release of identification with the drama. Very quickly, his soul was expanding and soaring on the wings of bliss and joy. Yes, I could remember myself, that being released from incarnation, especially in a dense physical place like this, can be the most incredibly expansive and liberating experience imaginable. If people can only learn to let go and be present, accepting what comes with grace and without fear, then the day of their death, *could in fact be the greatest day of their life!*

It is for no weird reason that the Dalai Lama invites people to contemplate their death daily. Why? Because he's morbid? No, *because he's liberated himself from the fear of it.* This means that crucially, he doesn't fear life either - whatever may come. It occurred to me, how important it is, that we help change humanity's vision of death: to accept it more as a 'passing on', which first has the feeling of coming home, and then leads to another life. Providing that is, you pass on without too much fear; providing you can let go of attachment as you progress through it. And unlike what I hear in the spiritual mainstream, I'm not one who subscribes to the idea of the soul being automatically immortal. *You become immortal by becoming self-realised, by moving beyond all identity with the physical universe.* I certainly know of, and have observed, souls that had become too infected by attachment to the physical, being *'dissolved back into the Source'.* I remembered, for example, it could happen via the passage through a black hole: a method by which dense karmic energy is broken down into consciousness elementals ('strings' as science would put it). If the soul is not progressing on the journey of evolution, and layers of karmic energy are released from a particular reality system (a planet like Earth for example), then the soul can be drawn through time and space, with that energy, into the black hole and fragmented down. I knew I had witnessed this many times.

Whilst it's deeply saddening to lose any soul, whenever it happens, I remind myself that the soul is not what we are. We are the inviolable, eternal presence - *the Source* - from which the soul arises. The soul itself is a stream of consciousness; a flowing wave of experience of the One. It can ebb and flow. It can rise and fall. But the One never fades away. Like I said: immortality as a soul is open to us all, *but you have to work for it!*

This knowing helped me greatly, as I began to encounter and remember the full horror of the Intervention, because I knew that the universal cleansing process meant that souls would not be eternally locked in some never-ending nightmare. The universe has its way of unlocking those experiences, no matter how dense and convoluted. This especially helped when I began to realise the momentous scale of the problem here: *it occurred to me that practically every person I encountered, and sat with in meditation, had energy implants, which entities were manipulating through the field. What's more, the vast majority were completely unaware of it.* In these early times, it also struck me how amazing it is, that people are carrying this karma around with them, yet often unseen, unconscious. For me, it provides the most powerful evidence of ETs, UFOs and the Intervention - way beyond the scientific. Do they really exist? The problem is that many are looking in the wrong place - *you have to look within and peel away the layers, because that's where you'll find them. Let's be clear: what's happening on Earth, is a full scale invasion; a war on the very consciousness of humanity, to which the majority are pretty much oblivious.* I came to realise that Homo Sapiens is actually an engineered product of this Intervention - *which is so interwoven and entwined in his psyche, that most don't even know when they're acting for themselves, or when it's being done for them!*

In those early days, I still had to pinch myself frequently, bringing myself back into the Source; reminding myself who I really am, and that the rest of it is just a drama, a story. You can't ignore it because it affects us all - we have to keep transcending, working through it, so that we may unravel it from our consciousness. It also helped to remind myself that this Intervention only occurs through lack of consciousness, and therefore it is serving a valuable purpose. When we learn to work with it, then our attention is drawn to our innermost blind spots.

The Team helped me greatly through this intensely challenging period of re-familiarisation...

> *How ever horrific these experiences are at times, the experiences themselves are not who we are. We are the inviolable Source, and it is the karma of the Original Mistakes - of lack of awareness - that created the drama into which you're now regressing. And living through these experiences, is the perfect way to release identification with them, to know yourself as the One.*

And so this is what I would do: no matter what horrors I'd encounter (through past life regressions), I'd remind people *they're just recalling a story.* For example, human women giving birth to demonic looking, hybrid creatures that frequently resulted in excruciating death for the woman. It became clear to me, that this is actually quite widespread within the human karmic story - *endemic to Homo Sapiens.* It explains exactly why there are so many challenges within human birthing and sexuality today; it's why so much healing is necessary. Often, people don't want to confront the truth, which I can completely understand; but I'd say to all reading now, it is only the truth that can truly set you free. When you can look into the eyes of your fear and not shrink back, then you - *as a soul* - can expand through all things, and thereby become eternal, immortal. It's this level of mastery which we're now being offered, as we evolve into the next form - Divinicus. And it is this path through the fire, that will be the making of us.

I wanted to know more about this Intervention, so I could help people deal with it; I knew it was a key purpose for me being here. The magnitude of it was steadily unravelling, right before my eyes. I seemed to know so much about it, and how to work effectively with it. *"Just where had I seen those black, almond-shaped eyes?"* And as I focussed on them, suddenly they were there, around me, trying to get inside my head: my very thought process had opened a channel to them. *"I know you,"* I thought. *"I know all about you, and I'm not in the least bit afraid."* Instead, I looked intently into them, with will and resolve, which they clearly didn't like at all, because in a flash, they vanished.

I started having many close encounters this way. Frequently they'd try to lead me astray, to pull me from the path and get me to do things that didn't serve - *for example, to get angry or judgmental with others.* It was through this, I learned something crucial about dealing with them: *as I embodied soul, standing firmly in my space without judging others, but then looking back into the source of the judgment - into their eyes - they'd back off.* It became clear to me, that stealth and deception are their key allies. They want you to be distracted, to keep looking outwards and blaming the cause of your problems 'out there'. They don't want you to look within. That's why the distraction of modern technology and entertainment is so prevalent in the society they've created. *But when you penetrate the veil, when you become comfortable and accepting in your own skin, the veils fall away - they become naked and powerless.*

As humanity begins to cross the karmic threshold into the higher paradigm of Divinicus, more and more people are having these kinds of experiences and past life regressions. It's amazing how interlocking and overlapping they frequently are. The pieces of the human jigsaw were now beginning to land ever faster. For me, even though the evidence of tampering is so abundantly clear within the human chromosome configuration, this past life evidence is still far more compelling. These experiences bring it home to each of us, personally. Yes, they're etheric, and yes, they require some interpretation - so they're not straightforward. But nevertheless, even though you might not be able to grasp the full details, it's clear you're carrying powerful past life influences in your field. In fact, as I so often say, it's not the details that matter - *it's the influences of the karmic energy that do.*

In this regard, I've become exceptionally careful not to unduly lead people, as I help them regress into their past life karma. I'll often see what the other is experiencing, but I've learned only to use this as a guide to ask the right questions - *it has to be their experience that's being relived.* And when you truly experience them at first hand, there's simply no debate about their authenticity. More and more people, through varied experiences, are pointing to pretty much the same story: *that of an Intervention within humanity's natural evolutionary path.*

Such regressions are far from easy. It's understandable that people might want to avoid them in the beginning. But each time people processed karma with me in this way, it always resulted in an incredible infusion of light and expansion: *their souls could embody more; they would feel more real and alive; profound psychic gifts would activate for them; increasingly they came to know themselves as who they truly are, which nothing could surpass.* By now, I only had to sit opposite someone, and consciously tune into them for a few seconds, before I'd feel their karma as if it were my own; seeing all manner of visions and flashbacks. It's a profound gift I came to cherish, which could only ever have happened by first confronting and cleansing away my own karma.

At this point however, I still can't say that I'd forgiven the entities who were responsible for the trauma that had taken place. I still couldn't claim that I fully understood it, nor why they'd done it. Some while after a spate of such regressions, when I was sickened to my core, and thought I'd taken all I could, I was practically on my knees praying for a deeper realisation that would relieve the sense of burden. The following day, I found myself digging in the garden; I needed to replace some of the wooden structures supporting our vegetable-bearing raised beds. As I split away some of the old and rotten wood, it exposed a nest of birthing ants - an entire colony, now furiously scrabbling in their shattered world. However, I didn't immediately empathise and explore their fate, because the urge in me to get the job done overrode deeper sensitivity.

In fact, I unearthed several colonies that day. All the while, the objective of needing to fix the structures for our essential food production was prevalent in my mind. Only with the final colony, the last piece of rotten wood, did I slow down and feel what they must have been experiencing (to some degree at least). I watched as some scrabbled to carry away their exposed eggs; others ran furiously up my spade and onto my arm, biting as hard as they could, to fend off this merciless intruder.

Then it suddenly hit me: in that instant, *I was no different from the Opposing Consciousness.* I had an objective, which in my model of reality seemed aligned. I was making some kind of blind, unconscious judgment: *that my reality was more important and essential than theirs.* The fact that the ants were not self-aware, seemed to make it all okay. Subtly, I'd accepted the judgment that they were less important than me: that's why I'd overlooked their plight; it made it alright.

In that instant the penny dropped - a flash of realisation happened. I understood a deeper aspect of the Opposing Consciousness, including other life forms, that control and manipulate:

> In their reality model of the universe, at their current level of evolution, humanity was just like the ants: a life form of lower awareness to be exploited and used. And in its industrial food chain, humanity does much the same to sheep, pigs and cattle.

I looked down at my spade, my hands clutching it, the ants still furiously biting at my arms. Tears welled up in my eyes: just as I asked for forgiveness from the ants, I felt I could begin to forgive the Opposing Consciousness.

With forgiveness comes deeper understanding. You peel away finer levels of separation and judgment. Even more of the universe unveils before your eyes - that which you can only appreciate after the density of inner judgment dissolves. This karmic pain is on the path to Divinicus, *the rise of the divine human*, and there's no avoiding it, if we are to continue to evolve. However, there's nothing to fear from it: the contractions of karma, when properly dealt with, always expand into something more whole and complete. Incredible gifts of insight and sensitivity become open to you, once the veiling density has been removed. It means that you can really appreciate - *perhaps for the first time* - what is actually going on in the field, all around you. Not just the magnitude of it, but most importantly, how to transcend it. The Intervention is afraid of you knowing the truth, *because the truth will always set you free.*

All was landing. But something still tugged below the surface: just where had I seen those black, almond-shaped eyes before? *Be patient my dear friend, for all will be revealed!*

10

The Matrix

"You have to know intimately where the physicality will try to own you: where the crassness of the matrix drowns out the translucency of the crystal clear."

Since the early hours of my incarnation, I knew that in some way I would be able to help unravel this Intervention. And that many others were incarnating here too: in fact an army of starsouls who had the power to nullify the effects of what was going on; they could help other souls reconnect back to the Source. First, however, I had to fully comprehend the magnitude of the problem. For example: how the field all around us - *the matrix* - is configured with vibrational frequencies to limit and disempower. Over time, we'd help Benevolence unwind it; but first, we had to get to know it.

Berlin is a truly fascinating place, and especially in an energetic sense. It was from here of course, that Adolph Hitler controlled much of the world during the Second World War. Perhaps what's less well known about the Third Reich though, is their obsession with the occult. In particular, they believed there had been an Atlantis, in which the Aryan race had been seeded from the stars. As I understand it, their agenda was to re-acquire the ancient knowledge and energetic power, in order to regain their previous 'glory'. And so they researched compulsively, many of the ancient archaeological sites, digging for clues. It's probably why there are still a good number of artefacts in the Berlin museum.

When I visit these places, I don't do it with the intellect. I'm not a tourist in that sense. I don't limit myself to 3D eyes, but allow sensitivity - through my energy body - to unveil the bigger picture. We're living in two worlds, not one. The higher plane is much more subtle; it lands internally as a vibration or an erudite knowing, and can only be realised once the coarseness of materiality has been mastered. You have to know intimately where the physicality will try to own you: where the crassness of the matrix drowns out the translucency of the crystal clear. Just like painting a landscape, it requires not only artistry, but also patience and persistence - honed attentiveness. Certainly, the fully awakened state of Divinicus, is not for the switched-off or lazy.

It's a feeling I love. It's real. Alive. I'm sure you know it too: the senses are bristling, like a fox's twitching nose, testing the air for the scent of the quarry. *Which way now? a dart of the eyes, focussing of the ears, there goes the hare, there's the direction.* That's the energy you're scanning for. What does the moment want to reveal now? Where's the story within the story?

It was with this level of honed attentiveness, to which I'd become accustomed, that I entered the Berlin museum in early 2012. It was late winter, with a cold frostiness hanging in the air, crystallising the breath, and chilling the skin to a faint tinge of blue. But as I entered the grand Victorian archway of the main entrance, the goosebumps were not just caused by cold, there was a palpable nervousness that gripped my gut, unleashing a rippling wave of nausea through my solar plexus: key tell-tale signs that something was amiss. This is what happens when you've peeled away the crusted veils of society's desensitisation (*encompassing the implants I discussed previously*). Invaluable information steadily reveals to you the deeper significance.

The mind's completely open. With no judgment of what you want to see, or any hint of the obligatory '*what you should see*', your field can work unhindered. The pull activates immediately, drawing me towards the staircase, and down into the basement. It became immediately obvious why: it was loaded with ancient Egyptian sarcophagi - immensely dense works of art, which held incredible depths of energy. It was like the throbbing vibration of a power station, generating a vortex of dense, pulsating energy all around.

It distorted and sucked in my field, just like putting a magnet next to a TV screen, causing the image to distort and contract down. It made my legs slightly weak, knees almost wanting to wobble. But you let it happen, because these are the tell-tale signs of your craft; these will help build the deeper picture.

It amazes me how easily people are drawn in by this sense of 'iconisation'. To the eye, they are shining wonders of the world, the subject of a zillion tourist snaps; but past the mind-level distraction, is an unmistakable energy, which you're affected by whether you know it or not. When you are sensitive, you at least have the power to neutralise its effect: to feel it, but then penetrate it; to expand through and beyond it. You have the power not to be disempowered by it. It takes energy, attention, and above all, the type of clarity that has moved beyond judgment, because you've actively felt, tasted and tested, *every contraction.*

So this was the base frequency aspect of the matrix that the Opposing Consciousness had initiated, using the densest stone to harness and hold the vibration; one that lowers and effectively whitewashes your own base frequencies. It works by destructive interference, an undercurrent, usurping your own wave with a deeper, more impulsive one. When you know it's there, if you maintain one Divinicus eye on it, then you can work with it. Reality is, after all, created by where your attention goes - the observer amplifying the authentic flow.

The base wave is not the only string in the bow of this Intervention. Having re-educated myself to this particular frequency, it was clearly time for the higher penny to drop. Again, it wasn't that I was intentionally seeking, the soul in me was simply expressing itself; unleashing one of its key characteristics. This time it was the Ray 3 (as outlined in Five Gateways): that of rationalising authentic reality; the decoder/translator. It was coupled with the Ray 5: "the scientist"... *Why on Earth does the field feel like this? Why does it debilitate so? And, being the catalyst that I am... How can I unravel it and bring the field back into harmony?*

Having moved beyond mind-led intention, I find the natural catalysis of Divinicus draws me into these situations, exploring the energetic avenues with the inquisitiveness and rebelliousness of a feral cat (*fortunately one with nine lives!*). The next frequency quickly engaged my energetic 'whiskers': this time it was a higher one - softer, subtler, but no less impelling. As the energy drew me upwards, through the museum, energetic hotspots leapt out, painting the underlying picture; curiosity was sweeping me along, attentiveness marking the spiralling flow. It felt like I was in some kind of energetic coil. But it wasn't until I rounded the final corner, and my eyes caught the 'head', that it dawned on me:

The entire museum, from an energetic standpoint at least, was laid out like a coiled snake.

I think it was the eyes that struck me first: dark, compelling, *almond-shape*d; and yet I also sensed a compassion in them. The mix of emotions certainly rendered any immediate judgment impossible. I guess that's what made her all the more alluring: a beautiful face might launch a thousand ships, but true captivation - *one like this* - raises as many questions as it answers.

As I was to discover on a later visit, it was almost certainly no accident that the museum was laid out in this way. It bore all the hallmarks - *the calling card* - of occult Black Magic. The matrix indeed has many interwoven layers; *but it takes the compliance of the covert, human hand, to fully anchor it.*

At this time, I'd not been made fully aware of that particular occult frequency. The memories came back in a way that enabled me to grasp the magnitude piece by piece, layer by layer. So as I tentatively entered the final room, containing the head that I'd seen from a distance, I became transfixed by the eyes - *those of the museum's coiled snake.* And as I stood directly in front of her, something ignited within me...

*Almond-shaped eyes, in an exquisite and alluring bust:
Nefertiti - the wife of the Pharaoh Akhenaten; stepmother of
the boy king Tutankhamen.*

I felt the echo of some ancient fear, that somewhere in the distant
past, I'd had to embrace and overcome. It stimulated memories
of an old foe, a cat and mouse chase through the ages, one that I
knew I had come here to resolve. *Who were they?* It doesn't take
the genius of a Dan Brown novel, to uncover the hidden code,
and remove the veil from the family tree: a starsoul family, often
written about in alternative texts - *the Annunaki.*

That very word alone opened floodgates for me. A close friend
was with me that day, also highly energetic, also extremely sensitive
to the underlying vibe; he too had experienced the past Annunaki
history at first hand. At this point, the energetic connection
between us was foreshadowed, or at least I was noticing it less. It
was the energy of Nefertiti that was luring me in. But as I drew
close to the glass display, my friend came back into the periphery
of my side view. So I noticed as both our attentions were drawn
simultaneously upwards towards the roof.

Above her head was a dome, and at its centre an unmistakable
grid. What was its purpose? Two things seemed to be happening:
firstly, the energy of my soul was being pulled upwards, such that
I had to refocus inwardly to prevent it; secondly, there were other,
subtle vibrations that were confusing the field - a background
'noise' that distracted. All was far from clear, but at least one thing
was certain: I would encounter again this strange 'over-grid' in
other archaeological locations around the world. For now, the
impressive character of the Pharaoh's wife, practically overwhelmed
any deeper sensitivity...

*And this is the key: distraction takes your focus away
from the source of your own creation, from your own
empowerment. When you're distracted in this way, you're
closed off - blinded - to what may influence your field.*

As I stood there in front of the glass case, although only a bust, it nevertheless had an aliveness to it, perhaps encapsulating an authentic energy of the queen. I could easily see how people of those times - *indeed any time* - might worship the glamour. But I'd do her an injustice if that's all I reported. There was a softness with her too, a compassion, to which the reported history bears witness.

Her husband, Akhenaten, was, by all accounts, more lenient, more liberalising; a democrat amongst the Kings. He featured the same elongated head of many imperialists from that time. In my knowing, it's a DNA attunement, making the overall bodily frequency more impressionable and controllable by the overshadowing Annunaki. It makes these 'blood-lines' much more susceptible to the 'right' frequency. Yet during Akhenaten's time, there had been rebellion. He'd ceased to worship the Alien 'gods', and instead, encouraged attention more to the Solar Logos - our sun. *Perhaps this was why he was cast out? Perhaps this was why his body was not entombed in the Valley of the Kings? Was Nefertiti anything to do with this rebellious leniency?* As I looked into those alluring, yet compassionate eyes, it felt good to think so. It seemed right. It was not the first time that I'd felt the presence of a regal soul, born into the heart of the Intervention, overtly suppressed; used to carry out a purpose, yet radiating a quiet compassion, the faintest touch of which, could break the strangling chains and liberate a soul. Like some kind of double agent, the face of Nefertiti definitely carried two sides.

I had felt it with Magdalen too, and later in 2012, I would taste it again with Isis. My heart felt momentarily heavy with the burden the divine feminine has had to endure. Was it even possible for a man to fully empathise with the challenge such level of surrender has taken? To overcome 'the beast', by first allowing it into the very sacred parts of oneself: to become almost a part of it, yet still to find yourself in it; to find compassion and forgiveness as the temple is desecrated. I'm sure there are countless unsung heroines who've incarnated here, working in such a way. It struck me immediately, why it's not possible to 'lower the bar' for Divinicus. We're all seeded with the possibility of Ascension into this divine form, but it's only going to be attained with the deepest and fullest inner inquiry. Not one stone of denial must be left unturned; no inner retraction must be ignored.

And so the journey drew me onwards, ever deeper down the rabbit hole: *how had this matrix become so endemic within society?* The Intervention clearly needed the acquiescence of the human hand to secure it in place. I yearned to comprehend, but above all, I wanted to bring the full depth of the surrounding matrix out into the light, that we may speedily unravel it for the good of everyone:

> *We have to be careful and have patience. You have to understand that the matrix has many interrelated frequencies to it. Practically every system in society: the energy supply and the industrial food chain; business, politics and education; they're all supported by the surrounding energy field, with minds and souls plugged in. There's also people's karma, which needs to be activated steadily. Were the whole thing to collapse at once, then you'd risk chaos. We must confront and unwind the layers one by one. Then, as many as possible will need to deal with the Intervention - inside themselves.*

> *So be patient my friends, and trust, for all will come!*

11

Liberty, the Bringer of Light

*"Trying to control reality is ultimately a fruitless task. It is self defeating.
You can manifest the field for a while, but just as the shackles
around Liberty's feet break down, failure is inevitable."*

The sky was sunny blue, as the tourist boat chugged its way steadily across New York Harbour toward Liberty Island. With little or no expectation, and an open perspective, tainted only marginally by the ubiquitous cheap gift paraphernalia, my heart began to noticeably quicken, as the boat turned towards her and Liberty came spectacularly into full view.

She is majestic, rising heavenward from the bay - a glorious design and an amazing feat of architecture. She has warmly greeted many a weary immigrant, to the welcome shores of the United States. And, despite the chequered history that has befallen many there, especially in these challenging times of profound change, she still towers like a colossus of freedom - one which many have tried to manipulate and control.

What I hadn't realised before, is that she is steeped in symbology. Adorning her head are seven bolts of light, which to me, clearly represent the Seven Divine Rays of Consciousness that form the soul-ray-harmonic for a person (written about in Five Gateways). With torch held aloft and constructed entirely of copper, she stands like a lightning rod, bringing in divine energy. And as that energy channels its way down through her body and into the ground, broken shackles are cast off at her feet. Yet the symbology doesn't end there: *she stands on a base, shaped as an eleven pointed star, a most awkward construction; like an afterthought, that doesn't belong. How curious.*

As I sat close to her feet, the highest powers of Benevolence were with me, and with their help, I was being reacquainted with the eleventh density. We were reflecting on the many different ways in which you can move energy. I was rediscovering that the most powerful of all, was to make myself open; to allow the natural flow to simply happen through me. In this way, you become a selfless instrument of the divine, and ride the wave of magical mystery through life. However, there are people, *secretive groups and societies*, who would prefer to control the flow, for their own base desires and intentions. In this way, they are simply replicating an Original Mistake of consciousness. There are groups who use numerology to help weave their 'spells'. Like the number 11, which in many ways is woven into the history of the Big Apple. Who will ever forget, for example, the startling afront to liberty, that 911 represented?

The Team were on hand to help me self-realise the deeper significance of this numerology: eleven also happens to be the number of dimensions in the universe. Imagine the Universe as a multi-dimensional apple. Some call it the "Torus". As the dimensions rise in vibrational frequency and increasing lightness of density, reality brings you ever closer to a direct experience of the Source: of pure formless presence. Here on the edge of the Void, energy is so light, and moving at such a high vibrational frequency, that reality searches out any slightest degree of imperfection; any disharmony resulting from lack of self-realisation.

You're now realising life faster than the speed of light: you can look anywhere in the universe and see what's happening, as if you are there, because in a way, you are! But if there's even the slightest judgment, or lack of understanding of what you're witnessing, then immediately density is formed around that thought. You're touching the edge of the spinning vortex at the centre of the universe - the core of the apple - but the disharmony means you can't hold that vibration. And so, like a playground spinning top, the density casts the matter formed around your confusion, right back down to the first density, to create manifested life once again. Thus you play out your distortion, until you realise the truth through it: you're creating at the speed of thought, or rather, the distorted convolution of thought.

The density you create by the lack of self-realisation, needs to play itself out again in a lower form of reality. Thus, through the spinning vortex of the Void - the core of the apple - the eleventh density becomes the first once more; they are intimately interlinked. The universe is a truly miraculous configuration of self-realisation. It is astounding. Literally breath taking.

In effect, what's happening, is that 'mistakes' of unity awareness are creating eddy currents of density within separation awareness. Matter is thus formed, within which, a soul must then embody, in order to play out the distortion, until realisation happens once more. You cannot have separation awareness without unity awareness in the same place - the two go hand in hand. Hence, you have the metaphor of the 'fallen angel cast out by God': a soul descends and incarnates into the distortion, until it releases itself from identification with the illusion. It thus self-realises that aspect of reality, on behalf of the One, and ascends once more.

I was contemplating this at the feet of Liberty, and quietly smiling to myself. It's not some vengeful bearded guy, high up on a white cloud doing this! It's simply the natural process of self-realisation, playing out in the dynamic of the universe. And there she was, standing magnificently before me, the 'fallen angel': Liberty - *Lucifer - the bringer of light through the exploration of darkness.* With torch held aloft, the symbology could hardly be more stark: *her feet stood on an eleven pointed star, yet the shackles of mis-representation lay shattered around her ankles.*

It seemed to me that Liberty is an icon of mixed messages: on the one hand, she's a channel of light. But one that's also been owned for distorted and twisted means: one that's been harnessed for selfish desires. For a while, this veiled deity will play out the distortion of the control; she is literally a manifestation of that in the field - that is her role. It's what she does: *she manifests the distortions and density that people contain within; she brings them out into the light, so that we can see the mirror of ourselves.* All manner of control can be wound around her as she works through the lower self-realisation, within which, she knowingly gets caught. She allows herself to play out her role - *whatever humanity might need.* Then at some point, realisation happens: the deity Lucifer is healed - *the satanic veil falls away* - and the soul reintegrates. As the distortion is unravelled, she rises once more. Thus she has provided the potential of self-realisation for all those drawn in. It quickly became clear to me, that her incarnation here - *especially in the place of the Big Apple* - was indeed all about control.

As these realisations landed, Benevolence began to 'speak'...

> *Trying to control reality is ultimately a fruitless task. It is self-defeating. You can manifest the field for a while, but just as the shackles around Liberty's feet break down, failure is inevitable. Why so? Because ultimately, all encompassing power rests with the flow of the entirety itself. Therefore, if you try to adopt a position, if you try to intentionally manifest, for a while you may create an eddy current of energy in the stream - some form of distorted manifestation. But what's mostly misunderstood and therefore overlooked, is that the eddy current and the stream are one. Thus as the eddy builds, it begins to draw the entirety of the universe towards it, ultimately to unravel it. Imagine it like building a dam to block the flow, except this stream is never ending - infinite. So no matter how high you keep building the dam, you always draw more and more water to push against it. Ultimately the dam breaks, and sweeps the blockage away. It is inevitable. It's just a question of time.*

(I go on to share the effects of this universal phenomenon called "Great Realignment" in more detail in chapter 19).

Unfortunately, despite this universal truth of the irresistibility of the natural flow, due to their lack of understanding, it hasn't stopped people trying to control life. Throughout human civilisation, there have been priesthoods and shadowy occult groups - secret societies - that have used 'black arts' to try to control the movement of energy for selfish motivations. For a while, it may appear as though they're being successful; for example in society at this current time, where it is well known that covert groups shape reality for their own particular agendas, hidden behind cloak and veil. When you look back through the karmic record, you can clearly see that the highest echelons of some such groups, have been responsible for some of the most despicable and heinous crimes (against life) imaginable. Yet even these are still playing out the Original Mistakes, that over time, are being unwound and reintegrated. No matter how far a life-form strays from the Source, to a truly benevolent energy, there is only ever forgiveness, reintegration and Ascension. Even the 'fallen angel' - who manifests the mirror of inner darkness - releases the satanic distortion, rising once more into the light.

Although these groups are well known to Benevolence, it does not feel right for me to point the finger and bring greater attention to them. They are, after all, merely the outward manifestation of humanity's karma: lack of personal sovereignty, handing over responsibility and self empowerment to others. As Sapiens evolves into Divinicus, and the Ascension unfolds in its fullness, such groups will dissolve naturally. And I have no desire to delay that realignment by maintaining the polarity of judgment: 'us and them'; 'right and wrong'; 'good and evil'. To me, there is no such thing as evil. People do things only according to the model of reality they hold. Whatever they have done, it is simply life confusing itself with the illusion, and then realigning itself back with the Source.

And I would say to those who might judge them, it is self-defeating, because to do so, is to create disempowering limitation within oneself. Just as the entirety of the flow is ultimately destructive against anything that would try to resist it, so too is it all forgiving. It will embrace lost aspects of itself at the point of surrender, and bring those wayward fragments back into the universal fold. The Team facilitated greater insight...

When reality began to take form, a part of the Self became lost within the multiplicity, consigning itself ever more to the sense of isolation from the 'all that is'. "Adam", was tempted by the 'deceptive snake', ate from the apple of materiality, and lost himself in the illusion. Of course it took some degree of misunderstanding and lower realisation to do it: judgment of the experiences that had been created, and therefore identification with them.

There is a great purity to the angel we call Lucifer. Lucifer was the light: a highly evolved soul that was sent into the darkened recesses of material experience - the density and isolation - to manifest the outer reflection of distorted thinking; to create the mirror in which mankind could rediscover itself. You have to manifest your inner darkness in the outer world, that you may shine the light on it, and thereby release it. It's an incredible sacrifice for any angel to bear.

If we can look into that mirror, be tempted into selfish, exploitative and hateful living - resist - yet not judge the mirror or others in it, we would always penetrate - with love - the darkness. It would simply fall away. Or, as you witnessed: explode into light. This is what Lucifer helps us see. She creates the darkness we hide within, inviting us to evolve beyond it; and she will not shy away, no matter how fearful the experience. Instead, like the divine feminine she is, she'll open: allowing the darkness of the beast to enter her; and, with her non-judgment, in the end, the unconditionality of her love will be felt. It's a love that melts away even the hardest heart. So it is the Angel Lucifer's role to fearlessly go into the universe's darkness, where other angels might yet fear to tread.

In the minds of men, Lucifer was judged: an idea was created - the deceptive snake called "Satan". And for a while, Lucifer judged herself, forming a limiting identity around that idea; she allowed herself to be a part of the controlling agenda. We can bite from the apple of the tree of knowledge, taste the joy of its fullness, yet when we get owned by it, and try to control it - instead we get controlled by it. The dream becomes a nightmare. Instead, we have to keep bringing the experience of the separation - of materiality - back into the completeness within. Then we can have our apple and eat it too. This is mastery.

So how can there be experience at all, if we don't consign another soul to the darkness of hell?

It's a good question. Of course there is no hell. Just as there is no heaven. Judgments have been formed of these words and illusionary realities created, in which, souls get trapped. When you are isolated from Pure Presence – from God – you are in hell; likewise, if you consign yourself only to the padded cell of bliss. What we're learning to do, through the experience of life, is to shed the limiting snakeskin of judgment. There is neither 'good' nor 'bad'. Instead, we find the sense of 'rightness' in the moment - that which is aligned with the natural flow of the universe, moving to ever higher harmonies. When all sentient beings, in all corners of the universe, have mastered this, then the universe will come into a state of Nirvana: balanced and harmonious flows of experience, without attachment.

My heart was melting yet deeper with acceptance and understanding. During my stay in the Big Apple, these facilitated realisations were shining from me, and into the field. Thus the Team reconnected with the wayward Lucifer. And it is with great joy that I can say - *through a catalytic self-realisation process* - I witnessed her healed and released back into the light. In short, she had judged herself by the actions she had been party to. But truth is the most powerful tool in the universe. Since everything is formed of consciousness, truth can unravel and reconnect even the most wayward heart. With understanding, forgiveness and love, Lucifer's shadow self - *Satan* - was dissolved: lost fragments of soul buried within the distortion - *within the matrix* - were healed and reintegrated.

It became abundantly clear to me, that those who called on her previously distorted power, would in time, steadily lose their grip. They will undoubtedly resist a while longer, with all manner of 'false-flag' events designed to instil fear. It may even be that these secret societies manage, to some degree, to fulfil their much spoken of 'New World Order'; in many ways, it has already been with us for some time. But although they still have an abundance of physical strength and resource, it's clear to me, their control over society will progressively unwind over time.

Crucially, what needs to be hoisted on board, *is that the bridging - spiritual - connection, of these distorted human groups with the Intervention, has now gone; the source of their spiritual power has been realigned with the divine. Thus, no matter what they might come up with, as society fractures and reshapes, they will steadily lose their grip, as the Ascension unfolds over time. The shackles at the feet of all those truly seeking liberty, were at this point, well and truly broken.*

What remained to be experienced next, and thereby animate a message to be shared widely, was the healing, liberation and **repatriation** of those various inter-dimensional entities, that had formed the other end of the bridge.

12

The Head of the Cobra

"We, your gods, have created you. From the humble hominid, we the Serpent People, have made you king of the Beasts."

I flew into Egypt late December 2012, knowing that my trip would in some way coincide with the realignments going on around the solstice. But exactly what, and how, I did not know. Egypt of course, is a fascinating place, not just because of its antiquity and archaeology, but also because of the revolution in 2011. You could say it was at the anvil of a popular uprising across the Middle East. It's no surprise, the region has always been an energetic convergence point throughout history: it was in this hot-bed bottleneck, that Homo Sapiens stepped out of Africa; not to mention where Neanderthal met his demise. I couldn't help but think the two events were linked: that much of the ethnic conflict in this region - the challenges, the complexities, the intolerances - were all karmic reflections stretching back into Sapiens prehistory, and the 'marshalling' of mankind.

It is the foreign currency of tourism that keeps modern-day Egypt afloat. Or at least it used to. The violence of the uprising, and the opportunistic influx of dogmatic religion, have made it a dark, dirty and dangerous place. I'm reminded that when you stir up the sediment at the bottom of the well of grief, the water is going to get distinctly muddy before it clears. Egypt is currently slip-sliding towards the very brink of the abyss. As tourist dollars dry up, there are precious few means for the people to scrape a meagre living, from the dusty and barren desert. Even the very attractions that lure people here, are falling into decay and disrepair. This, the foundation stone of current civilisation, is a great mirror to all of society: *without exploitation of both the land and the people, the system does not work; at some point, no matter how embedded that inequity is, something just has to give.*

Nowhere could you feel it more strongly than on the streets of Cairo. It had become a hotbed of revolutionary protest. Appropriately, Benevolence had picked for me a beaten up hostel, a hair's-breadth from the apex of Tahir Square, the centre of much of the unrest. *"Thanks!"* I inwardly projected. *"You're welcome. What better way to feel and empathise?"* came the patient but firm response. I'd walked through war zones before, and this possessed all the latent chemistry to ignite another flaming tinder box: religious zealotry, poverty, frustration, anger, worthlessness, and hopelessness - all essential ingredients of the molotov cocktail. You could drink it in through the air, activating waves of anticipation and nervous expectation. There's a need to tread very carefully indeed - *"Just like walking on eggshells, Grasshopper!"*

Somehow, I could feel the link to the pyramids, across the other side of the city, in Giza. It seemed those foundation blocks of modern society, had been the source of this division: this control and manipulation, which could only be contained - *sarcophagus like* - for so long. At some point, no matter how heavy the coffin lid, the light of day would shatter it, and toss its broken pieces aside. It felt like that was beginning to happen, here, in Egypt.

Of course the Giza Plateau is visually stunning; that is, once you've traversed the festering decay of the broken communities on its doorstep: *how the once mighty have fallen!* They rightly say: 'pride comes before a fall', and pride would have played a considerable part in the construction of such megaliths. I can clearly recall, sitting near the temple of the Sphinx, at the entrance to the Giza Plateau, marvelling, as the throng of eager tourists wound their way up to the main attraction: the three pyramids sitting on top of the plateau. The Sphinx was clearly well placed, as the tourists passed reverently by. What an incredible beast to keep watch, to impress and persuade: *what could it be saying I wondered?*

As the thought wafted into my consciousness, like a stirring breeze, I was sitting side-on to the mysterious lion-shaped creature, with the wave of tourists winding upwards behind me. The Sphinx construction is nothing short of miraculous in human terms. It had been cut from the surrounding sandstone bedrock. Apparently, according to modern-day Egyptologists, it had been hewn out with very basic hand cutting tools. The 'waste' blocks so cut, were then positioned with rope and pulley, to form the Sphinx temple. *Really?*

They commonly used *two hundred tonne blocks,* cut with the finest precision, then lifted more than forty feet into the air, supposedly by block and tackle. Really? I find the idea simply incredible. It's been shown that a team of twenty experienced personnel, working with even the most advanced modern-day cranes, could not position the blocks in such a way. To me, it is practically certain, that only some form of advanced technology could have performed such a feat. Either early civilisations were much more sophisticated than the history books show, or else we can only speculate, that highly advanced, external 'help' must have mastered it. At some later point, surfing the internet and allowing resonant inner feeling to land realisation, this particular penny dropped:

> polarity - every atom possesses it. Reverse the polarity through the application of appropriate sound technology and you don't have to lift a thing. Levitation can happen by reversing polarity within the molecules of the stone. The block is then repelled from the natural polarity of the Earth. It literally lifts itself!

You can just imagine the impact on the already mightily respectful Egyptian population: *"Gods"* - there would be no other appropriately reverent term. And so what about the Sphinx itself? What message might it convey? It would appear that the original form has been masked with a touch of reworking, by some slightly egotistical Pharaoh! What better statue on which to imprint your likeness? But look from the side-on: is it really the face of modern man? It certainly isn't: the lower jaw protrudes much too far forwards. Indeed, the proportions are more reminiscent of an early human, perhaps even Neanderthal.

Now that's fascinating when you consider the symbology: the head of an early human on the body of a lion, adorned with the headdress of a cobra. As the endless weave of tourists continued to wind their way upwards behind me, my eyes narrowed, and I slipped back in time. What might the Sphinx have said to the local population as they passed respectfully by?... *"We, your gods, have created you. From the humble hominid, we the Serpent People, have made you king of the Beasts."* And of course unsaid, but quietly implied: *"We are your masters, bow to us, and we will bestow upon you the divinity you desire."* Why would they not make their way reverently up to the 'Great Pyramids'?

I'd sat inside the second pyramid at the beginning of the day, to gain some reflective quietness, before the tourists arrived en masse, in their brightly coloured coaches. Unless you're already half dead, the pyramids simply cannot fail to impress. They're a stunning testament to incredible building skills, astounding mathematics, and deep cosmological knowledge. Those who built them, were no simple peasants. Far from it: the three main pyramids are aligned exactly with the four cardinal points (North, South, East, West); the proportion of the height to the perimeter of the base, is the exact same as that of the North Pole to the Earth's equator. Amazing! How, at the time, could they have known these dimensions?

It gets even more impressive: inner measurements contain not only the mystical figure of pi, but also the speed of light (yes indeed!); and, according to impressive pioneering work by the alternative researcher Robert Bauval, the three pyramids are aligned exactly with the belt of the constellation Orion, as it was in 10,450 BC. This in itself is fascinating for two key reasons. Firstly, contrary to traditional Egyptology, the Sphinx itself was more likely built, not in the fifth millennium BC, but rather the 11th millennium BC, just after the end of the last Ice Age, as the flood waters receded. It's been clearly shown in the weathering, which could only have happened through intense rain - exactly the conditions at the end of the Ice Age in the 11th millennium BC. The second reason, is that in 10,450 BC, the constellation Orion would have been at its lowest point in the sky, in what's known as *"The Precession of the Equinoxes"*. Clearly, this was another important milestone to the ancient Egyptians, and whoever guided them.

The pyramids would have been capped in gold, a super conductor of energy, and this is what activated in my awareness next. As I sat in the centre of the second pyramid, millions of tonnes of focussing rock directly above my head, I could feel two distinct effects happening: firstly, there was a low base frequency, which seemed to draw my lower soul vibration down into the earth; secondly, there was a higher frequency, which seemed to separate my higher self, drawing it upwards into the Fourth Density. The effect was probably only a mild ripple of what it would have been, with the gold keystone intact. To knowingly understand what's really going on, you'd have to be very sensitive to your energetic field; you'd also need an advanced degree of integration between your higher and lower self. In other words: you'd have to be either enlightened or pretty close. If, on the other hand, higher and lower self were not fully integrated, you wouldn't notice the separating effect; a subtle shift into the higher frequencies would probably feel quite blissful. Plus, you'd activate various healing and psychic gifts - a window would be opened into the 'heavens' so to speak. Except this would not be integration *with the higher densities* - bringing them down inside yourself. It would only be an illusionary bubble, in the Fourth Density. Clever. Very clever indeed.

And what about the various 'star channels'? Cut with pinpoint accuracy, one in particular is directed perfectly down from the constellation Sirius, and another, from Draco. Perhaps it was meant as a clue, to where the Serpent People - *the Annunaki* - and others in their 'alliance' (a theme I'll return to later) actually descended on humanity from? Maybe the pyramids were also meant as channels of energy, and as locating devices for inter-dimensional travel between the locations?

As these questions and realisations landed, I had the strong urge just to leave. Being in the heart of the pyramid, encased under millions of tonnes of energy-harnessing stone, made me feel pretty unwell. It was like a more intense version of standing directly under an electricity pylon. So I gingerly edged my way back along the very small channels toward the entrance. Unfortunately, by now, a long line of tourists were scurrying their noisy way, *ant-like*, through the tiny, claustrophobic corridors towards me. It delayed my exit, and with that, intensified the feeling in my solar plexus.

No doubt about it, I was very much relieved to get out and drink in the fresh air; to feel my field reharmonising, integrating and centring once more; to experience the tightened coils in my gut unwinding and unravelling. It was a welcome relief indeed. Yet, I could imagine that for those already pressurised by a society of control, the activated Fourth Density connection would feel pretty impressive: the frequencies radiating through the pyramid, might well heal the hybrid human body; but it's still a hybrid, with submerged, disempowering frequencies - just as billions are desensitised today, by excito-toxins and electrosmog.

One can only imagine - *or regress into* - the ceremonies that took place within the pyramids: what light might have been harnessed; what energy channelled through the gold capped apex? Certainly, it would have been enough to propel a soul up out of the body, and thereby out of the dehumanising pain. Thus, I can imagine, the Egyptian slaves would have felt contrastingly quite expanded, and liberated, from their daily toils. Of course they'd be pretty thankful and subservient to the 'gods' that had 'helped' them. Maybe they thought they'd been rendered divine by the process? It's a theme I'd witness directly, at first hand, later in the journey.

*You have to wonder at the enormity of it: just 13,000 years
of technological 'development' later - practically the blink of
Gaia's eye - and yet the Serpent has almost complete control
over society. Who would have dreamt it?*

The Giza Plateau was overcast that day, with an almost reddish
smog. But as I was leaving, just for a few minutes, the smog parted
directly over the second pyramid, the one in which I'd been sitting;
a space opened for a few welcome rays of sunlight. Indeed, it was a
curiously shaped hole in the clouds: *looking very much like the head
of a snake.* Sensing I was about to be shown something important,
my attention focussed keenly. As two smaller clouds drifted across
the open gap, there was simply no mistaking it: now, with its two
eyes staring down from the heavens, the synchronistic pattern
in the sky, *looked very much like the head of a cobra.* My pulse
quickened, and as I squinted to look closer, the head morphed into
a spacecraft, from which shafts of light were beaming down towards
the pyramid's apex. Yes, it was my perception, but I'd certainly not
created it in my mind. It was a higher-dimensional 'conversation':

*In no uncertain terms, I'd been shown the head of the cobra
- exactly what its purpose in society was - and, still, very
much is.*

The Team made it abundantly clear to me, that the time had
come to unwind this unwelcome Intervention, to 'strike off' the
head of the snake. The knowing was strong in my heart, that
Benevolence was gathering to facilitate this. It was also clear from
other experiences I'd had in Berlin, that at least some elements of
the Opposing Consciousness alliance - *the Annunaki, represented
by the cobra's head* - were now ready and willing to leave. It seemed
they had accepted their destiny to heal, evolve and realign with
the Source. '*But how would that be facilitated?*' I wondered. The
Valley of the Kings, containing underground tombs of many of the

Pharaohs - *those who had so worshipped the Annunaki* - beckoned strongly. It was clear that there was something wholly unsavoury about the mummification process, and what it was designed to do. It was time to confront and release some of that decrepit energy; time to release the head of the cobra.

Fascinatingly, as my taxi driver explained, whilst precariously negotiating potholes, dips and bends at breakneck speed, many other tombs had been discovered of 'ordinary' people on the approach roads to the Valley of the Kings; tombs that were now being unearthed and cleared as a result of the revolution. As we whistled past them, it seemed wholly synchronistic: *a modern-day revolution was unwinding not only today's authoritarian rule, but also the energetic foundations buried deep within the past.* I marvelled how amazing it is, that history unravels through spiralling cycles of consciousness; ideally always ascending into ever higher harmonies of alignment.

As I entered the Valley of the Kings, although I wasn't sure what to expect, I could already sense the stench of the decrepit, needing to be cleansed and released. Yes, people may marvel at these 'wonders' of the past, but sadly, mostly without a truly inquiring heart and mind. First, I had to fight my way past the inevitable clamouring hands of the trinket sellers, and the tourist buggy drivers *(surely, I couldn't possibly walk the couple of miles around the valley without getting tired or lost?).* Finally, I found some space and quietness just inside the entrance, so I could truly listen and feel. This is what the Divinicus in us so often really yearns for - *some peaceful quietness to really sense the energy.*

At a cursory first glance, the valley is visually stunning. As I scanned around me, its steep sandstone walls encased its buried artefacts like an amphitheatre. But dig deeper, and it feels like some ghoulish testament to the long gone. In fact I've never been to a place that was so energetically dense. Even the Berlin museum was just a shimmering sound bite of this real undertone. The high and rocky valley sides held the deep booming resonance perfectly

- clearly their intent. And buried underfoot, eons of Black Magic density: so much so, that it felt like being trapped in some force-field, making my body heavier and legs weaker... *I thought maybe I might need that tourist buggy after all!*

Why go to so much trouble to embalm their kings? If you pass on into the 'afterlife', what need of a mummified body would you have? I guess that would depend entirely on what afterlife you were intending. These were the early human bloodlines of the Annunaki - human 'avatars', that could be more easily influenced and acted through. As I came to rediscover later - *and thereby deeply empathise with* - the Annunaki were a race that had been in terminal decay since their unfortunate disconnection from the divine eons ago. As I stood at the entrance to the valley, with this thought resonating in my mind, I was flashed back to an earlier experience in Berlin: an apartment steeped in aristocracy, and at the time, still bound by the threads of some dark energetic secret.

If you know what you are doing, it is not hard to open portals into higher dimensions. You just need the will to do it, an anchor on each side of the bridge, and enough of a deep consciousness feeling to connect the two. This 'feeling- bridge' can be done with either the surrendering love of the divine, or the control of an intensely desired agenda - *some twisted alien root.* Beware if you're intentionally manifesting: *what energy are you really tapping into?*

I realised early on, that it was a part of my purpose here to connect with the Annunaki. I simply knew, deep within my being, that we'd shared some common story; on different sides of the proverbial 'fence' yes, but definitely some shared history, which was only now beginning to emerge from the fog of the dim and distant past. *I could feel them.* And whilst I was rightly deeply cautious, there was the sense of pity and empathy in my heart too.

It became clear to me, that I was to form one side of a reconnecting bridge, so that Benevolence could convey a message:

whatever synthetic reality you've become lost in, and are now losing others in too, it's not your fault. You're playing out one of the Original Mistakes - that of Controlling Realities. You've been isolated from the divine, and it's now time to come home.

However, it wasn't a message that could simply be spoken, and thus easily ignored. As I would soon rediscover, their belief in their distorted reality was deeply embedded. It was so painfully entrenched by traumatic events in another constellation, that had happened many millions of years ago; a catastrophe, which caused their sense of isolation from the Source. The Annunaki had been set adrift in space, *abandoned by God*, and as far as they were concerned, surrendered to their fate of creating synthetic, substitute realities. Despite the suffering I knew they'd caused to countless millions of people, my heart was slowly but surely, beginning to soften towards them.

I came to realise how important it was that the message be conveyed first hand; I knew it was a purpose of my incarnation. As risky as it had been in the past, I nevertheless had to allow them deep within my psyche: a benevolent 'trap' had to be sprung, to lure them in; to show them that nothing could ever surpass divine connection to the Source. No illusionary reality would ever suffice - 'God' abandoned no one. It had to be experiential, to achieve the greatest impact. So, as challenging as it was, I opened my heart to them and surrendered myself on their altar. I allowed the snake to slip surreptitiously into my psyche, and yet all the while, kept trusting that the divine could speak, quietly but surely, through the deception. The 'trap' was sprung.

The Fourth Density works either by 'allowing', or by 'intent'. You can either allow in the higher flow and be a willing amplifier for it, or you can shut it out, focus awareness and shape it according to your desires. For the latter approach, the strength of intent is the key to success: the more focussed you are, the more successful you will be; you have to be sure enough, in your mind, of your intended creation. But herein also lies its critical weakness: if a thread of doubt is introduced, because the force of intent is ultimately shown to be lacking, then this doubt can quickly go viral; it unravels the intent like the rapid expansion of a broken watch spring. It's simply a question of time.

As paradoxical as it may seem, there's nothing so remotely powerful as surrender and vulnerability. It may sound completely contradictory, but when you're intentionally manifesting, there's always the loose thread of doubt. If, however, you've been trampled into the dust time and again, if you've watched your dreams and aspirations being mercilessly trodden underfoot, your heart shattered, and the will to hang on shredded, then ultimately, if there's real letting go, you surrender into the Void - the place of infinite potential. You realise the inevitability of your being - your destiny - and **nothing** can thwart destiny, providing that is, you've removed everything in the way.

> *I'd say to anyone reading, whenever you might feel the invasion of psychic attack, as challenging as it may seem, surrender is the key to success: not resisting the invasion and thereby making yourself a bigger target; rather, becoming as nothing in it. In which case, it has nowhere to strike. What's more, you can now resonate that thought/feeling frequency of forgiveness, leading to reintegration with the Source.*

So I was standing in the entrance to the valley, opening a doorway back to Berlin and into their 'hive'. Whereupon, they came into my consciousness, tempting many allurements, embellishments, grandiosities and glamours. Some of which, in the past, had succeeded (like owning my soul identity "Open" with supportive manifestation). Yet a truly honest and inquiring mind, will always spot where you've gone astray; where you're building up ego, rather than paring it down.

On the threshold of this 4D portal, I remembered a time when I'd died and passed into the 'afterlife'. I thought I was going to 'heaven'. That was at least my expectation, and the initial sense of bliss and light had fooled me. It's like drinking a vintage bottle of wine, you feel happy and carefree with the first couple of glasses, but then the deeper you delve, the headier this Bacchus aftertaste becomes. It was indeed more expanded than the 3D, *and that was its allure*. Yet, just like the alcoholic crutch that keeps many going in the desensitised 3D, so this padded cage generated the falsehood of a more liberated 5D - a temptation of expansion to lure you in. A false energy bubble had been created, like some giant amniotic tank, maintaining a perpetuated life, limited in time and space.

I'd been contained in this limbo for an unknowable period. As with the broken wristwatch, time had vanished, as had practically all my sense of self. I felt many other souls around me too, contained in other bubbles, partially of their own making, yet all serviced by the Annunaki. It was a purposeful deception. In that world, souls have great value and can be 'harvested' for energy, for embodied experience, for implantation, for possession.

Mind control keeps you there. Like the 'drip, drip, drip' of a television soap opera, they play back to you the subtle echo of your own limitation, your own judgment, your own attachments to 3D life in the physical; your own fear of letting go, of being infinite. It might be the connection to a partner, to a lifestyle you'd once had, or once desired.

I wasn't an easy prisoner. My soul continually questioned the legitimacy of it, and so ever grander deceptions and allurements were needed to keep me there. Eventually, the grandest trick in the book was rolled out: *I was the "Messiah"*, holding a very special frequency in this very special place; a very special love and light to help guide the flock home. How many people on this Earth, have said they were Jesus? How many people in churches the world over, have reached out and '*touched his face*'? How many people are now disempowered, by the longing for the return of their '*saviour*'?

I bought the Messiah illusion for a while. It's probably a bit like winning the lottery: you've wanted something all your life, something tantalisingly out of reach, yet always with the taster, the promise that keeps you on the treadmill. You land the jackpot, all that new spiritual glamour, it's going to change your life forever. How easily we're limited. I guess every soul has its price... for a while.

But in this virtual amniotic sack, as the snake seductively whispered its allurements in one ear, so Benevolence channelled its piercing questions in the other. You see, this is the true power of Benevolence, *and your inviolable power as a sovereign being.* It is not about providing the answers on some silver platter, downed with a spoonful of sugar (that's how the opposition do it); it's all about the limitless power of self-realisation, delivered through an appropriate question...

> *"How can a Messiah lead anyone home, if home is already in your heart?" "How can you be saved, when there is nothing to be saved from?"*

It's only an ego that needs saving, one that buys into the illusion; the very idea that you need saving, is enough to separate you from the Source. To the needy, it's like a meme that goes viral in your psyche. But when you know in your soul, that you don't need saving, that which you would be saved from, pops like a fairground bubble.

And as you escape, as you find true liberation, you correspondingly sow the seeds of doubt within the very mind that would control you: the interrogation is turned full circle, back on the interrogator; they see their own limitation in your ecstatically free eyes. It's like a game of chess, there may have been countless moves on the board, but it's only by the final *coup de grâce,* that you know checkmate has been delivered. It was in this way, that Benevolence spoke through me. I had risked all, been sucked in and deceived, yet in the unravelling, the question of doubt had sown a viral seed within the minds of our oppressors. How long could they hold onto their fear-based realities? Just as the Berlin wall seemed, for many decades, like a permanent fixture, I could already feel the foundations beginning to waiver. Surely it wouldn't be long before the wall would topple?

They had tempted me with a final false reality: the Earth 'healed' with high technology and 'free' energy, but ultimately, only a perpetuation of the current status quo. In response, I rippled the awareness of the inevitability of flow, realignment and unravelling, expressed through every cell of my being. In my mind were pictured two possible paths. The first: reconnection to the Source; acceptance of the boundless, reharmonising co-creativity that selflessly serves the betterment of all. Then there was the alternate path: hanging on, twisting the coil ever further; ratcheting the density, until the inevitable 'crack'; then being sucked - whirlpool like - into the black-hole abyss at the core of our galaxy. The first path had a future; the second would result in compaction to super-density, then exploding into shredded elementals... *This was no negotiation. Unless the snake surrendered to the flow, it would shed more than just its skin!*

So they came to me for a solution, an answer, but really what they were seeking - *as with all souls* - was the right question. First, they wanted to know on whose behalf I was speaking. I opened my being ever wider to the Group of Nine *(the Team)*. They knew them well; thought they'd dispensed with them way back down the path. And through our connection - *the bridge I was serving* - they were reminded: *that those who best know how to surrender, will ultimately succeed; no matter how long it takes, patience always persists.* I felt they really knew that now, and so respected the reconnection, feared the crystal clear clarity. But the Team wished them no harm. Quite the contrary of course: you never, ever, fight anything but yourself; therefore why fight? *Especially when you're looking in the mirror of your own creation, your own unconsciousness.*

The Annunaki wanted to heal. And they wanted me and the Team to empathise with their pain. But both sides knew, it would take much time and patience...*You don't heal 120 million years of trauma in a few hours!* And, although at times I can be slightly impatient, this thought adjourned the re-familiarisation until another chapter. With that, I was propelled right back to the present moment, standing in the Valley of the Kings, feeling the physical manifestation of all this negative energy, with my heart yearning to do something about it. But what to do?

At that exact moment, my contemplation was interrupted by someone calling me, from up high on the valley side. I ignored it at first. That's the problem with the Sapiens mind; it can be quite closed, poorly adapted to spontaneity. It's a direct reflection of the Opposing energies, which live by the ethos of a controlled and manipulated agenda. So the Divinicus in me had to hear once more, to be able to pinpoint the invitation for divine spontaneity. This time, it was in the form a young Nubian Egyptian Boy, calling me in broken English, high up on the valley side... *"Come Sir, I show you beautiful view of entire valley."* Yes, I could feel it, this was for me.

Still, I was caught in two minds. The taxi driver would be waiting. *What if he gave up and left? Ah that's just the fear-based Sapiens in you speaking. Why not let the trusting Divinicus live a little!* So I changed tack, and scrambled up the valley side towards the young Egyptian, perched on a ledge, waiting eagerly for me to join him. He smiled a soft, warm energy, and with an expansive arm movement... *"I show you beautiful view of whole Valley."* His articulate gesture, finally pointed to a pyramid shaped peak, a few hundred metres above us, a mile or so away in the distance. It looked amazing, but it would take at least a couple of hours arduous trekking, and climbing, to make the return journey. However, before I could hesitate, he'd suddenly turned tail and quickly headed off in the direction of the peak. What else should I do, but follow?

Arduous it was. Not to mention the close heat, the shale rock of the steep valley side would, at any moment, crumble and slide. Each time I considered how treacherous it was, my attention was drawn to the bare heels of the young Egyptian, wearing only sandals. I was reminded...*What one man can do, so can another!* Thus we wound our way precariously up the side of the mountain, sometimes climbing, sometimes scrambling, across the loose surface. *"Keep your weight moving,"* would ensure I kept re-adjusting to the ever changing and seemingly flowing landscape... *"Don't stay still for too long."* I reflected on how this approach had helped me many times, to see and overcome the Intervention, which liked only the slow and sure-footed certainty of predictability...

> *Spontaneity and flexibility are your true allies. It's how the flow works, and it's a complete contradiction to what the Opposing Consciousness is manifested for. So always, when in doubt, allow your natural spontaneity to decide for you what to do.*

After about three quarters of an hour, with me tired, breathless and sweaty, we reached the top; the young Egyptian on the other hand, looked like he'd been on nothing more than an after lunch stroll. Amused, I marvelled at how wonderfully adaptive this Sapiens vehicle can be... *Given the chance, that is. Given the space to find the true gifts of the Divinicus buried deep within.* As for any kind of 'prospecting', you have to put yourself out, you have to dig deep, and have the patience to locate those buried nuggets of soul gold. For a brief moment or two, I allowed myself a humbled self-congratulation - *perhaps I'd mastered a little more than I dare admit to myself.*

But neither is Divinicus about resting on one's laurels! So what was I here to do? What was the purpose? Indeed it was a stunning view, not just of the valley, but hundreds of miles across the Nile, North, South, West and East. I marvelled how you could see practically the whole of Egypt. Maybe not, but at least it felt that way, such a commanding view it was. To me, this was even more powerful than the sense of the pyramids: a seventh wonder of the world they may be, but no man-made construction will ever come close to the mighty hand of Gaia. I reflected that she'd humbled many a civilisation before, and would undoubtedly do so again. '*How foolish to challenge the natural force of Gaia*'.... This was the feeling that filled my heart, as I waited for the purpose of our ascent to materialise.

It didn't take long. When you're open and aligned, it seldom does. My attention was drawn to the young Egyptian: "*You take your time, Sir.*" His Middle Eastern energy, flashed me right back in time to the Sinai with Trinity, and an experience shared in Five Gateways, that almost cost her life. The soul of Chris had moved on, bar some energetic connections and filtering I still experienced. I was beginning to get increasingly familiar with this Sapiens form as the "Resurrection" kicked in. On the surface, we'd gone there for a holiday, but in underlying truth, the trip was more to activate shifts of consciousness in the Middle East. We'd experienced a powerful Opposing Consciousness Intervention. But in working to counter it, we'd established a multi-dimensional portal, to help release Earth-bound souls and bottled-up energy from the region. As challenging as it was, we'd mastered an invaluable gift, which I was to call on many times in the future. And here, on top of the pyramid-shaped mountain, overlooking the valley of the long-dead Kings, yes, it felt entirely appropriate to facilitate another energy-shifting portal.

It's so vital not to build these things by intention. Whose intention would that be? And how would you then draw the maximum energy of Benevolence? It's all about realising and first attuning to energetic density: feeling it, penetrating it, being consumed by it; until you become as one with it. Yet even in the consummation, there's still the light of your soul, untainted by it. This requires a great deal of skill: to have that level of empathy, such that you can penetrate the darkness to its very core, yet not be twisted, tainted or overcome by it. If you can feel it all, yet still channel and amplify the fullness of your soul-ray-harmonic, then you will be a powerful catalyst for change.

By then, I'd certainly established a wide open empathy. I could feel the energy of this blood-line intervention, a gut churning, that made me almost want to curl my toes with rejection. It tempts that kind of retraction, but it's exactly where we must soften and penetrate through; establishing empathy is essential to moving energy.

Next, you need something with which to ground higher cosmic energies of Benevolence. For this I'd been carrying something very earthy: an ancient spiral-shaped ammonite. I'd infused it with energy by carrying it in my hand, and opening my heart to the higher harmony of life, which I felt infuse through me as pulsating light. I found an appropriate crevice in which to plant the ancient fossil; it gave me the sense of foundation, connected to the core of the planet. It matters not the exactness of it, what truly moves energy, is a deep heart-felt feeling, summoned from the depths of your being.

"And so what next?" That's the intellectually unanswered question, you must then hold in your consciousness. Hold the question, be connected to the earthing anchor; now expand your consciousness up to the heavenly skies above, the question itself melting you into selfless divine service. The Divinicus in you knows this sense of absolute surrender, as a core aspect of its nature. This is the secret, this is the alchemy that truly unleashes divine magic. And so the energy began to swirl through me, then around me, building and building, swirling like a spiral, until it took the form of a gathering tornado. My attention was drawn out into the valley: *"See not just the material, but the lay of the multi-dimensional landscape."* I could sense the energetic dead spots, and the hot spots. I remembered: I could link the hot spots together, simply with my open awareness. Now, the swirling motion began to expand out into the valley, creating a spinning vortex, drawing the hot spots together, spiralling upwards, into the higher dimensions.

Where was this energy going to?... *Into the Angelic Realms.* Once you know the angelic vibration, once you can recall the experience of it in your consciousness, you can quickly open a channel across the dimensions. This is what being multi-dimensional is really all about. And I felt an immediate response: the angels were open to me; all I had to do was open my heart to them and ask. Thus the bridge was connected. The swirling, multi-dimensional vortex now had a destination and a very definite purpose. As I looked back at the dead energy spots, with inter-dimensional eyes, the vortex expanded its reach, swirling down to connect up the density; dislodging it like crusts of mouldy bread, eventually directing it through time and space into the Galactic core; there to be shredded into its conscious elementals.

And what of the Annunaki? They'd be reconnected with the Source: some would heal, evolve and ascend; others would rejoin the cycle of reincarnation. This was the next chapter for the Annunaki, assuming they'd acquiesce.

Thus the portal was opened, spiralling upwards in its mighty relocating power. Yet, further afield, I could still feel the final remnants of resistance by the Annunaki. Still something needed to happen. *What could it be?* The word *"Isis"* softly entered my consciousness. Clearly, the divine feminine was the next 'destination' on my journey.

13

The Divine Feminine

"Where tightness, fear and anger hold an island of position,
softness is the gentle flow that blends with it,
before washing it away."

I am a warrior by nature. But it took me quite a few lifetimes to realise, that surrender is the key to being a real warrior of life. Surrender is the key to mastering the moment. Even if you feel compelled to shake something up, unless you've fully empathised - *by feeling into the surrounding energy* - you can never really catalyse something. Yes, you might be able to force the outer circumstances to some modicum of temporary suppression, but the situation will always reform in some other guise.

Human society through the eons has been predominantly loud and brutish, governed by the horrendously distorted Divine Masculine. Brute force and ignorance have shaped the surface of our planet, riding roughshod over Gaia's soft forgiving lines. Like all women, she has had to graciously endure and accept this ungracious intrusion.

As I write this, I'm reminded yet again of the classic film, "The Matrix". The lead character, Neo, ("The One") has battled and fought tirelessly with his arch-rival, and satanic antithesis, "Agent Smith". In the closing scenes of the trilogy, Neo is finally beaten into complete submission, trampled into a desolate crater in the earth. The moment has arrived for the victor to assimilate Neo's consciousness into his being: not just to violate, but to totally consume; there is not one ounce of fight left in Neo's ravaged and shattered body. All he can possibly do, is surrender to his fate.

That fate becomes his enduring destiny. For as he is consumed by the beast, the surrendered thread of light softens into the very cells of the oppressor. Where tightness, fear and anger hold an island of position, softness is the gentle flow that blends with it, before washing it away. And so, although consumed within the darkness, the light continued to shine brightly. Anger and hatred cannot hold together in such a soft inner hue. Its very cells are shattered and blown apart. Thus, in the apparent defeat of the warrior, the Divine Feminine aspect of his nature ultimately shines forth from within, through the beast that had consumed him. The tables are turned. Darkness has nothing to hang onto and shatters. Light wins the day.

And so it has been the purpose of the Divine Feminine, to softly surrender to the Intervention here on Earth.

In earlier episodes of the journey, I spoke about Lucifer: the much misunderstood and maligned *Bringer of light through the exploration of darkness.* She was 'cast out of heaven', into the darkness, to be lost in identity: there to create a manifesting mirror to all around, that they might see themselves better; to rediscover at-one-ment and completeness with God. It's about being trampled on, and completely consumed within the darkness, becoming a part of it; holding that polarity, until the identity you're interacting with is blown apart. The ancient light of truth is thus found at the heart of each distortion, and is unwound, that the light can shine brightly once more from within.

That's why I therefore consider Lucifer a 'she': a being that the Team have sometimes affectionately called "Lucy"; because she has this surrendering feminine capacity within her very nature. There's still the divine masculine sense of purpose - the aspiration to change and catalyse by bringing others to the shocking confrontation of truth. But it is the surrender, that enables her to master her trade; to live and endure, the absolute separation from God.

I have felt her many times in my life. She's the angel that will creep up behind me in some darkened alleyway, and make the hairs on the back of my neck stand on end... *'You're not going to shirk away from this are you? You're not going to retract back into some protective shell? Come out and see the darkness that you've denied within. Come out and taste every morsel of it, for only then, can you release any fear and identification with it.'*

So this is where she's been much misunderstood. You'd have to be well along the path to get it. You'd have to be in a place where you're fully realising that to be confronted with your worst fears, and nightmares, is not a malevolent thing to do, but quite the opposite. Whatever you've hidden away inside in some darkened recess, you must take out and explore, so you can liberate the light from within it. Initially at least, most people can't handle that level of confrontation, that level of fear; so like some seabed mollusc, they retract back inside their shell, blaming the outer world in the process.

The Temple of Isis was misunderstood and maligned in this way too. It was (and still is) an establishment of High Priestesses (now in a higher dimension). They are Masters of Alchemy: *the transformation of base metal into gold.* And one stream of light, one method of magic, is through surrendered sexual intimacy.

The problem is, that the divine masculine has become so tight, so focussed, so controlling, that he has divorced himself from the deep sensuality of feeling. There wants to be consumption of the divine feminine, experienced as a ravaging - *an exploitation of -* to fulfil selfish, self-identified desire. It's that quick fix of release from the pain, to rapidly and forcefully ejaculate it into a soft, acquiescent receptacle. In such a state, the divine masculine totally loses himself. He's gobbled up the apple from the tree of life so furiously, he couldn't truly feel himself in the process. Now he just wants another apple. Ever so badly.

It's a tall order for the divine feminine. But someone has to do it. In order for this darkened distortion in the universe to unravel, it has to be be held in a non-judgmental, empathic and acquiescent embrace. This is the work of the Priestesses; the alchemists, using tantric mastery to render the masculine soft and pliable. As I would come to re-encounter, you have to be brought to the very edge of pleasurable identification, to the very place where you would lose your empowerment, in order to release yourself and once more find God. What was once merely physical 'bump and grind', now becomes sweet and sensual divine union.

Thus the Priestesses have committed themselves to allowing in the beast of man, that he may find the divine feminine inside himself.

Just like Magdalen, the Priestesses have been rendered 'whores and prostitutes', by judgmental eyes. Eyes that could neither truly see nor understand; eyes that were themselves longing to consume. Jealous, angry eyes, that didn't realise it was a lost aspect of themselves they were really hating: *that part buried so deep, they'd given up trying to find it again. In fact it is so buried, they don't even know what they've lost!* Although having been thus relegated to the backwaters of life, cast out by the ever-so-righteous religions, the Divine Feminine has endured, carrying the flame down through the ages, one day to be rekindled in the hearts of men.

The Divine Feminine was thus a great prize for the Intervention. If they could twist and distort, pervert and prostitute, they could provide a honey trap for the divine masculine. You can see its effects today, on every magazine stand, on street corners, in shopping centres, on the internet and TV; soft porn, it's all-pervading, a debilitating judgment of divine union, dehumanising women, and the men who exploit them.

I recall shortly after my incarnation here, walking onto a garage forecourt, past the newspaper stand, and there, in the corner of my eye, was a semi-naked woman adorning the front page. Large breasted, curvaceous hips, pouting lips: her costume designed to titillate and to tease. How can a heterosexual male not in some way be distracted by that? And, if not distracted, then desensitised by it - owned by it. The 'perfect female', has been surreptitiously slipped into the human psyche, even when buying groceries or fuel for the car! And now nothing less will do: every woman is expected to conform to a particular image, a particular shape, a particular way of being, so that every man can be tempted and lured in. Whole industries have been created on this one, basic instinct.

It was abundantly obvious: the tables have to be turned. Distortion has to be dissolved, so that the Divinicus in the divine feminine and masculine, can be unwound, liberated. And so divine souls have chosen to incarnate here, in the most challenging of places. First to be ravaged and consumed - *to be 'assimilated into'* - so that emergence from such darkness, can lead the wayward back home. As I've previously explained, I felt Nefertiti was just such a woman, Magdalen too. And now, as I made my way south through Egypt, to the exquisite temple of Philae at Aswan, I could feel the soft kiss of Isis, blown to me on the desert breeze: she, the Goddess whose wings have launched a thousand myths. What magic lay waiting there I wondered?

Be patient my friends... for the veils of distortion will fall.

14

The God and Goddess in You

"And we must continually remind ourselves, that in a similar way to this Egyptian tragedy, we are all actors in an often glamourised theatre, where consciousness is simply seeking to unravel itself through appropriate 'avatars'."

In Egyptian mythology, Osiris was a god, who governed with his goddess wife, Isis, by his side...

> *But there was great jealousy and rivalry for the throne. Set, his brother, deceives Osiris, sealing him into a casket and setting him adrift on the ocean. The distraught Isis embarks on a pilgrimage, eventually finding him. But then Set murders Osiris, cutting him into fourteen parts and distributing them at various locations around the Egyptian Kingdom. Isis, beset with grief, finds all but one of the parts - the phallus - and resurrects him minus the physical aspect of his manhood. But, having attained deity, their son Horus is immaculately conceived by the couple. Horus then battles with Set, killing him, to take back the throne.*

It's a myth which dominated much of ancient Egpytian theology and society. The full story, described in copious detail, undoubtedly contains great symbology of the times, and also possibly represents the spiritual journey itself, with some of its various transitions along the path. For instance: the deception and distortion represented by Set; being lost in the sea of emotions; the aspirants search to reclaim their divinity represented by the grieving wife; the soul fragmented into physicality; spiritual resurrection and divine creation, leading to rebirth of the God within; thus, in a heavily distorted and Intervention controlled society, the story may well have had some Benevolent influence too.

Certainly it was of phenomenal importance to ancient Egyptians, who invested incomprehensible effort in the construction of the pyramids. Which, we've already seen, included the pinpoint alignment to Orion - *Osiris* - the hunter; and the star system Sirius, representing Isis. So are these meant to be our Gods? Is that what the Egyptians were shown? Were these 'deities' placed here by the Sirian Annunaki and Orion Greys? Inescapably, I was now arriving at the resounding conclusion... *Yes!*

As I've constantly intimated throughout this journal, you cannot control consciousness indefinitely. You can manifest the most monumental illusions in the universe, the greatest fictions, but the sword of truth will always eventually pierce them. To a truly inquiring eye, all veils will ultimately fall. I've also spoken of how the divine feminine has, so often, helped break through internal self-deception; by allowing assimilation into the tightened darkness, to explore the nooks and crannies, before bursting through with light. And to me, so is the case with the goddess Isis, who, as I came to discover, worked first *with* the Intervention, and then *against* it.

It's very synchronistic, that earlier in Chris' life, he had a poignant encounter with Isis, whilst rowing at Oxford University. He was an excellent oarsman, of modest stature, but great skill. Sitting in the stroke seat, he could weave a rhythm that could blend separate parts into a much greater whole. But his physical stature, being somewhat less than the usually large oarsmen, meant he was denied a place in the prestigious "Blue Boat". Instead, he had been relegated to the reserves - *to row in "Isis"*. As I made my way along the Nile to Aswan, I pondered this powerful metaphor. You see, the stories are there in our lives, if only we care to look beyond the surface level. To me, it said: *human destiny was thwarted and denied; we were born to a lesser god; one put in place for us by this Opposing Consciousness, that had diverted us from our true greatness.*

I hasten to add, that just as with Nefertiti, there's a deeper side to Isis too. Yes, she was an imposed Goddess, established as an icon - *a Marilyn Monroe* - designed to tempt, to tease, to allure and therefore to distract; to dehumanise those who were all-too-ready to lose themselves in the illusion. But she is a benevolent soul, to me, a '*double agent*', placed at the very heart of the Intervention, steadily influenced by Benevolence, and brought back into the light. In the story, Isis took pity upon the plight of humanity, and began to help them out of their servitude. I'd not met the Isis deity yet, but I could already sense this as being true; just as others of the Opposing Consciousness have changed sides, reconnected with the Source, and are now working with the light.

If I look back at the story of Chris, yes I could say his destiny had been thwarted - he had not become a full Rowing Blue - because his full potential was not recognised. His real capability was not about individual strength, but how he might bind together otherwise disparate rhythms. Yet, he himself would admit, that he had measured success by someone else's yardstick - *by society's judgment* - of what it means to be 'successful'. Success is where you find it - *when you discover and learn something deeper about yourself.* It has nothing to do with adorned accolade, rank and award. It's about fulfilment, of you as a soul, feeling the fullness of your expression - *all the soul's frequencies* - way beyond the baying crowds. Yes, humanity has been deceived, but deceived by his own karma, his own lack of consciousness. It's what he needed - *to be allured by the physical temptation of separation* - to be dehumanised, lost, so he could find himself on the journey back to divinity.

And so to me, Isis has always played this benevolent 'double agent', within the battle of consciousness, born into the heart of the Intervention, in a leading role. Despite the desperately influencing density in which she finds herself, the aligned consciousness in her core activates; she deeply empathises and helps reclaim the humanity within men. That to me, is the metaphor which has been so eloquently handed down to us.

And we must continually remind ourselves, that in a similar way to this Egyptian tragedy, we are all actors in an often glamourised theatre, where consciousness is simply seeking to unravel itself through appropriate 'avatars'. It is through this interplay, that the illusion of life is made real.

It was with this in mind, that I sat in the fallucca, gracefully gliding across the Nile, with the early morning sunshine gently kissing my face, my heart beginning to flutter, as the temple of Philae drew ever closer. Yes, there were mixed feelings. I knew Isis had been a part of the initial deception, that had led humanity astray in this ancient civilisation; but I knew she had greatly helped too.

My arrival at the temple coincided with a motorboat full of tourists, who fortunately, all trotted off clockwise around the island on a preplanned tourist trip. The pull for me, on the other hand, was clearly guiding in the opposite direction - first to an open-roofed temple, with huge columns, directing one's attention skywards. As I stood in the middle, opening my heart, the energy came quickly flooding in: it was a soaring, lifting and lightening sense, that rapidly expanded me. Reverence and gratitude naturally swept over me. I had made the connection: a bridge that would now guide me through a multi-dimensional experience of this amazing place; beyond the merely surface level.

When I made it roughly half way around the island, into one of the main temples, sure enough, I met the throng of tourists, busily snapping and chatting. But by now, a good part of me had slipped into the space between the spaces. I could see and hear them, but their intrusions were faint and dreamy. Like ghosts in a far off distant place, they weren't really there.

In one of the back-rooms of the central temple, which was beautifully adorned with Isis/Osiris hieroglyphs, I felt to sing: a chakra meditation, which directs energy through each of the chakras sequentially, from the base, up to the eighth chakra, and then back down. Yes, there were tourists drifting in and out, but in this divine envelope, they seemed inconsequential. I'm not a bad singer at all, but it's funny, how, when the heart pours out divine love, it has the effect of clearing those who are still uncomfortable with it. And so very quickly, I had the chamber all to myself.

I was singing to my heart's content, such that I didn't notice the small, dark-skinned, Nubian Egyptian now standing at my shoulder, beckoning to me. As I looked into his eyes, an instant soulful connection was ignited. Unlike the tourists, he had effortlessly accessed the space I was now in. He was suggesting I follow him, which felt good, so he led me into a smaller, hidden chamber, which I could see was usually closed off to visitors. This place was the most divine of them all. Much smaller, it had the feeling of completely enveloping you. It was deeply transcendent, even the hieroglyphs seemed to morph off the walls and dance in the space with you.

The chamber was different from the others in many ways, but especially because of an aperture in the centre of the roof, opening out into the clear blue skies above. Now, I understood exactly why the Nubian had beckoned me here: this is where I should sing my chakra meditation. Which I did, with heart-felt gusto.

Sure enough, the expansion was immediately magical. My soul was quickly soaring on out-stretched wings. And I was not alone: a divine presence had joined me; a vibration I had known deep in the past. There was an unmistakable feeling of recognition, yet it still took some time for the energy to filter down into my mind, that I may grasp its identity. Finally, there was no mistaking her: *it was none other than Isis herself.*

A merging of souls transpired - a joyous dancing in the heavens. As a telepathic bridge opened between us, it was sublime, yet tinged with a very slight discomfort, tainting the experience. It felt like guilt. I could sense it in the air. It was **her** guilt, and as the thought sparked in my mind, it became an open 'topic of discussion'. Except in this higher dimensional connection, there are no words, nothing so clumsy can be sustained here. It was much more the activation of 'knowing exchange': *a resonance, and an interplay, that causes pure, unadulterated knowing, to land in your being.*

A gilded thread of consciousness wound its way deep into the past, back to the beginning of the Human Intervention; back to the time of 'Atlantis'. That was where it had all begun. In my dim and distant memory, I'd known exactly where the centre of it was, *because I'd been there.* But at that time, I couldn't remember its exact location *(be patient, all will come!).* I knew it was where Original Humans had been downgraded: a sub-human species was created, yet on the surface, one that appeared more connected, more divine; a synthetic 'heaven' had been manifested by a sense of expansive vibration, luring the soul away from the Source.

Yes, I knew it now: Isis was at the centre of the Intervention. In some way, her consciousness had helped lure in and deceive the souls of men - *by playing a vibration close to the frequency of their own Twin Flame.* Now I remembered - it's a devious technique the Intervention have used (and still do) to distract internal attention from the Source - where one's Twin Flame is seated *(your Twin Flame does not incarnate; it holds the polarity of your soul close to the Source, drawing you back home).* Instead, a heavenly nectar, so sweet, tempted the divine masculine from his seat of empowerment - so he could be more easily used and controlled. In an ironic synchronicity with the Isis/Osiris myth, man had lost his manhood; and now I could clearly feel Isis' sense of responsibility.

I knew I'd long since processed and overcome any anger about what had happened. It had taken place because of cosmic karma: the Original 'Sin' - Revelling in Physicality - being too invested in the creation itself. It was simply not her fault: a theatre play had to be acted out; the players needed to take their part. As tragic as this tragedy was, human souls required it, in order to evolve and grow. Especially the divine masculine, who needed a vehicle in which to lose himself: to be thwarted from his rightful destiny - that of sensitive, divine connection; feeling the divine feminine in the physical, but connecting to his Twin Flame back at the Source.

I was able to hold this realisation in my consciousness, but not just as an intellectual idea; I'd deeply experienced acceptance and forgiveness. Not the shallow version, which is mostly achieved by denial: rather that which has relived and deeply penetrated the pain; one that has felt through every pore, the isolating trauma of dehumanisation. I'd reclaimed and reintegrated my soul, despite the experience of down-graded hybridisation; I'd integrated *through the Intervention*, not by fighting it, but by penetrating it with surrendered softness - the very divinely feminine trait I could feel in Isis now.

> *And I put it to you reading: this is how we can all overcome the trauma of the Intervention - by allowing the divine feminine to surrender us into, and through it. If you can accept it, to the extent that you become it, then paradoxically, you can transcend it; you are defined by it no longer.*

That's why I didn't judge her, why I *couldn't* judge her. I'd discovered a precious gift inside me, *exactly because of the deception; because of the Intervention*. I'd found the surrendering side of the divine feminine: a priceless gift that had somehow, somewhere, become detached from my experience; dampened and trampled into dusky inner layers. Back in my isolation, there had been nowhere else to go, except deeper inwards, always deeper down the coal mine; through the hard, dirty blackness, until eventually, I'd struck a seam of gold - *I rediscovered my Twin Flame*. That's why, that day, I could feel nothing but love and gratitude for Isis.

And I guess that's why I was able to be a channel and a bridge into higher consciousness, that Isis may feel forgiveness. It had to be someone having a human experience, yet travelled and expanded enough not to judge. *Of course, it needed to come from a man, nothing else would do for her.* It had to be from one of those, whom, in her perception, she had deceived. And with the forgiveness, there was first a deep recognition in her heart, followed by an outpouring: like a waterfall of love, in which I was now bathing... it was like sweet scented nectar *(but I was nevertheless still connected to my Twin Flame!)*.

It was a heavenly dance indeed. I know it may sound strange - *a deity having to forgive herself.* But a deity is evolved enough to know, that to truly forgive, to forgive oneself, is to be taken right back into the sense and sensibility of the feeling itself. Because feelings store energy, and energy has to be realigned, which the dance between us, and the bridge to divine union, was now fulfilling.

It was tremendously difficult to tear myself away from the chamber. The sanctum had propelled me into this deep multi-dimensional exchange. But everything has its conclusion. Just before I began to slip earthward once more, Isis made it known to me, that she was there - *through the ether* - for all men, who would honestly look into their compacted inner density; to reclaim the sensuality of the divine feminine - *and their own Twin Flame* - that which has been denied them so long. It also occurred to me, that the powers-that-be in society - *the dark occult groups particularly* - no longer have any effective call on Isis (no matter what manifestations they may try). Just like Lucifer, she had been realigned with the light.

As the fallucca steadily glided its way once more across the Nile, looking back at the temple, now disappearing in the distance, I contemplated just how many women have suffered through the ages due to man's ignorance. And more importantly, *just how many are here today, to recover him from his darkness!*

Back on the mainland, I found myself immediately drawn to a house, that of a craftsman who carved figurines, mainly in alabaster. Of course there were many of Isis, but one stood out strongly for me. As the light penetrated through the translucent stone, she looked like an angel with out-stretched wings. My eyes were drawn in closer. I noticed the detail of the feathers adorning her wings. Immediately, I felt Isis in my heart once more, and she was speaking to me: *"Each feather represents a frequency of being. When you call on me, feel deep into yourself, and look for a sense of authentic beingness - your Twin Flame - which may have been lost in the darkness. These recovered frequencies will sweep you up, into the out-stretched completeness that you truly are; like riding on the breeze of a desert levanta, flying on the wings of love."* I was deeply moved. My heart melted.

It was the last day of my Egyptian travels. A karmic journey had carried me deep into the past. I had recovered many gem stones, unlocked frequencies that I could now call upon. *And there remained an unanswered curiosity about Atlantis; but that would have to wait until further down the path.*

My home-bound aircraft touched down at Heathrow, and as I began winding my way back to Glastonbury, I had to pinch myself... *'Was that really the Goddess Isis, of myth and mystery, that I'd danced with in divine union?'*

I realised I couldn't know for certain. It was an etheric experience, logged within a fallible human mind. But then did it really matter? What matters most is the message I took from it, and the shifts of energy that I could palpably feel. For those reading, my experiences may provide a message of deep compassion and empathy, for all who've lost themselves in this grand deception, this grand illusion...

Perhaps then, there's an essence of Isis in all women, that can help recover the Osiris in all men?

These thoughts were prevalent in my mind, as I wound my way along the A303 country road back towards my home town, Glastonbury. It was the 18th of December, Chris' birthday; the all important winter solstice of 2012 was approaching rapidly. It was late in the day, darkness had already drawn its blanket over the gentle rolling countryside - the sky offering a clear canvas for the stars to twinkle upon.

It occurred to me, I would pass the ancient megalith and cosmic calendar, Stonehenge, on my way home. And as I crested a hill just before this magnificent site, I could hardly believe my eyes - *the car almost swerved off the road.* There, directly above Stonehenge, was the constellation Orion - *the Hunter Osiris* - resurrected in all his heavenly glory. It was absolutely jaw-dropping. It spoke volumes to me: *'that we possess the power to reclaim humanity from this Intervention, and restore his heavenly glory'.* My heart melted - the messages don't come any stronger than this.

15

The Ascension of Gaia

"Rise out of the destructive darkness,
through the Five Gateways,
to a renewed Earth in a
higher vibrational paradigm.
All are invited!"

Early in 2012, I'd had an awakened dream. A message was passed down to me. It was something like this: *"On the winter solstice 2012, the all important 21st December, you'll find a high place in Glastonbury, not the Tor itself, but a place overlooking the Tor. And there you'll be shown something powerful, a message in lights: its purpose to confirm for you, unequivocally, what's happening at a planetary level."*

I'd forgotten the dream, but later that summer, I'd had another poignant premonition. It was during one of the Openhand courses, in the height of the summer at Cae Mabon, a secluded, country retreat centre in the foothills of the impressive Mount Snowdon. We'd always had amazing gatherings there: always about a dozen of us, nestled on a wooded hill side, in ancient looking 'hobbit' houses; there was a bubbling, cleansing stream, jinking its way down through the site. The feeling was inescapable - it was reminiscent of the Shire, in 'Lord of the Rings'.

It was the perfect getaway, and yet paradoxically, the stillness of primal connection with Gaia, opened a space to take you deep into your 'stuff' - *your karma that is.* Collectively, we'd frequently had astral journeys through humanity's, and the Earth's, past history. We'd relived them in a feeling way, beyond the mind, such that there could be no question as to their authenticity. You may not have known the exact details, but the essence of what had taken place was unquestionable.

We'd had visitations from a number of deities, especially in the Sweat Lodge. Once, the Goddess Pele had come to us, the Goddess of Volcanoes, speaking of a time *(perhaps in the near future)* when the Earth's crust would heat up, become more malleable, and cleansing fire would burst through. Then afterwards, Gaia herself came to us: one of the empathic ladies took on her very consciousness; the energy guided a swaying 'dance' between us. Gaia was telling me of her karmic history, which I was able to relate back with some words to the group.

I'd experienced her, in the form of what I can only describe as, an early 'protoplanet', in the creation of our solar system, many billions of years ago. I recalled the much younger Gaia incarnating, but was shocked to the core, by the immense gravitational forces that she was having to endure. It was like the intense weight of her, was now crushing and condensing me into the floor. The pain was excruciating, my mind whirling like being stuck inside a giant washing machine. This was hell! I just needed to somehow explode out of there. And indeed Gaia did, shattering the planet she was supposed to take on, sending rock fragments out in all directions; forming the asteroid belt we witness today between the planets Mars and Jupiter. It was utterly amazing. I guessed cosmologists would 'die' for this experience! *(I'm also aware of other explanations for how the asteroid belt got there. Nevertheless, this felt entirely real and plausible for me)*.

I also felt Gaia's regret, almost a tinge of shame, if deities can still actually feel that. This was her destiny, yet her inability to handle such intensity *(understandably so!)*, had dramatically shaped her path and created cosmic karma that, at some point down the road, she'd have to re-encounter. Then suddenly I got it:

The matrix that had been created by the Intervention, was not just serving humanity's karmic need, but Gaia's too!

Initially that really shocked me. It sacrificed some 'sacred cows' I'd been holding onto. I'd always seen Gaia as being 'innocent' in all of this. Suddenly, I could feel the energy grid the Intervention had imposed, and the way she experienced it: controlling, low frequency impulses, like a constant droning; an intense irritation, that made me want to crawl in my skin, contracting down into my shell. This too was how Gaia had responded, and it shocked me to feel, *that she herself,* had all but disconnected from the Source - all but given up. 'Why had it been so drastic?' I wondered. The Team were on hand to help me realise...

The Intervention has taken a once beautiful Earth of great harmony, and turned it into a place of control and subjugation; oppressor and victim. In her soul, this is not Gaia's way, and for such a heightened empath that she is, it has caused intolerable pain. She can intimately feel the suffering of all her children, and the terrible imbalance.

Later on, I would get to understand the immense impact on her of the 'raptor consciousness' (chapter 18) and just what it has done to the Earth. For now, I saw in her past history with Earth, how she'd vented this karmic frustration several times. And how each event, each *'mass extinction',* had cleared much sentient life from the surface. My attention was propelled back to the zenith of the dinosaurs, as they rampaged across the Earth, spawning all different forms of new life, but mostly with one common thread connecting them all - *consumption,* on a gargantuan scale. Of course they were annihilated by an exploding comet - *what part did Gaia have to play in that, I wondered?*

Then I saw it: the soul yearning of Gaia to restore harmony and balance - with *an impetuous need caused by her cosmic karma.* It drew the comet - by the Law of Attraction - which brought their reign to a swift and brutal end. Now I could feel in Gaia the karma of regret she'd kept recreating: the pain and anguish of being responsible for the decimation of life several times before *(the five mass extinctions)*. This then, was the divine purpose of the debilitating matrix she also lives in. The point being, that over time, she'd manage such intrusions, the control of the Intervention, and be able to endure it; to accept it without needing to change it, *for only then can you truly process karma and move on.*

All of this I could see clearly, feel intensely, as I danced and swayed at Cae Mabon. Our 'tango for two', had opened a divinely telepathic bridge. And so what was the solution to it all?...

> *When Gaia had processed her karma, she'd no longer need the matrix; she'd no longer require the control drama we're all living in. Upon which, it could more easily be unwound from her Fourth Density energy field. The entities could be removed, and relocated elsewhere in the cosmos. She would ascend, centre herself in the Fifth Density, and build a new, vibrant reality, for all of her evolving children - those that could fully embrace the Fifth Density frequency of unconditional love and co-creative harmony.*

At that time, I got the strong sense that the wonderful work spiritual people have been doing across the planet, had greatly helped in this karmic healing of Gaia - empathically supporting the processing she needed to do. All she really needed now, was to send a clear message to her human children. This is what I felt back at Cae Mabon in the summer of 2012. I felt it would be a rebirth: Gaia would birth a new life in the Fifth Density, where other ascending life could join her.

As the gathering closed, Trinity and myself headed off into the heart of rural Wales, for some much needed rest and recuperation. It was the height of the summer, and although I seldom, if ever, watch TV, some undeniable inner pull, guided me to switch it on, at the Bed and Breakfast where we were staying that evening. To my complete surprise, the 2012 London Olympics were just beginning, *and that very night was the opening ceremony.* Imagine then, the look on my face as the ceremony unfolded: a mock up first of the Glastonbury Tor, the heart centre of Gaia, a stage set for many themes of human civilisation; you saw first how people had lived in olden times, before the rise of the machine, in self-supporting communities - which my heart yearned for now; we witnessed the onset of the Industrial Revolution, the wanton greed and destruction of our 'green and pleasant land'; we saw the various unnatural systems that have created society and subjugated life; finally, I could hardly contain myself, as *five golden rings* were hoisted above the rapturing crowd for millions worldwide to witness. Surely this had to be the message...

"Evolve yourself, then rise out of the destructive darkness, through the Five Gateways, to a renewed Earth in a higher vibrational paradigm. All are invited!"

Although clear as daylight to me, it was understandably a message lost on most - you have to be tuned into this synchronistic mother tongue of the universe. But I consoled myself in the knowing, that Gaia and Benevolence would provide many more messages and messengers in the years ahead. Life would not simply 'explode' here as it had done in the past; as many as possible would be given the chance to wake up and realign. But of course it would always be a choice as to whether they did.

Just a few months later, approaching the all important solstice, although I'd somehow forgotten my prophetic dream at the beginning of the year, I could nevertheless sense a clear build-up of energy in the field, mirrored through my own body. It's like my throat chakra *(which leads into higher dimensional living of the Fifth Density)* was constricted and constrained, creating a kind of 'pressure cooker' feeling throughout my body, all the way up into my neck *(I was empathically sensing Gaia)*. Other awakened people were experiencing it too, all across the world.

So in the days immediately leading up to December 21st, the

sense that a birthing process was taking place greatly intensified. As I made my way up the Glastonbury Tor for my early morning walks, the 'pot-bellied' shape of it, seemed to take on the very womb of the divine feminine; its soft, rounded curves made the hill look very pregnant. And the term *"Christed Child"* kept coming to mind. In this sense, "Christ" is referring to the catalytic Christ Consciousness, which is activated to help a necessary realignment - *a rebirth* - in the field. So the Christ Consciousness would help catalyse and activate the birthing of a new Gaia, in a new paradigm. It felt utterly momentous.

That said, although the build-up continued, I still wasn't sure what would happen on the all important December 21st - what would be manifested into our outer world? Many sceptics would understandably ask: *"Why did it have to take place around a particular date?"* To me it's a clear sign of the natural synchronicity of the universe: when life is allowed to order itself, things click naturally into place; the natural harmony has an authentic balance, with a strong degree of consistency. This is bound to express through signs and synchronicity: the universe's mother tongue, that we may all feel a part of the re-harmonising flow.

So like the shock of an alarm clock, on the eve of the 20th, a short time before midnight, my eyes sprang wide open and I leapt from my bed, guided by an irresistible inner force. I was going to be shown something of great importance, not to be missed. It was clear: when you're in the flow, there need be no thought; the Divinicus in you simply knows what to do. This is how living in the Fifth Density works. I was to collect a few friends, those closest to me, and take them out into Glastonbury. To where, I had no idea, but I knew the pull would carry me.

Wearyall Hill was the first destination - the mythical mound just on the outskirts of Glastonbury with a clear, uninterrupted view of the Tor. Legend has it that Joseph of Arimathea brought the young Jesus here, and when he landed on the shores of Avalon (Glastonbury was surrounded by a natural lake in those days), it was

Wearyall Hill where he first stepped ashore. Joseph is supposed to have planted his staff, made from holy thorn, which then sprouted, thus becoming a site of reverent pilgrimage for thousands of years. And you can certainly feel the benevolent energy on the mound today. It has a strong air of mysticism.

We made our way up the hill in the dark of night, surrounding street lamps lighting our way, the sense of magic hanging like a silvery mist on still air. It was Trinity who felt it first (she's a highly sensitive empath, able to take on the feelings of other sentient life as her own). It was just as if she'd gone into labour, carrying the weight of an unborn child in her womb. Her legs now decidedly wobbly, I had to support her with a loving shoulder, as our pace up the hill slowed to a wavering amble. Of course it was not her own child she was carrying, but feeling that of an unborn Gaia. Breathing heavily, muscles aching, and with barely controllable swaying, the sense of expectation heightened with each careful step, until finally, we made it to the peak.

It took a while to recover and centre ourselves, that we might then feel our purpose there. *What was the mission?* It has to be an open question, one that, like the silvery mist, just hangs in the air, with no contracting inner need of an answer. In that way, the Divinicus in you amplifies the build up of energy, interrelating with the background flow and the mirror of life all around. Now divine creation is beginning to happen through you, just by the open question alone; it's heightened observation, and keen attentiveness, that are the co-creators of life's magic.

I just love this hidden dialogue of life. It is so much more fulfilling than any surface level chitchat. Deep and meaningful, and always with a purpose, it will direct the open-minded with a heart-felt, telepathic knowing exchange. This is where inner intimacy is so vital: it's the blind seamstress, weaving together the inner and outer, into one seamless garment. You'll never get this with the mind alone, your cloth would be threadbare. You have to feel, with nimble fingers, each stitch of the moment.

And so the pattern begins to take form until, hallelujah: you've got it; you've seen just what it is, and what it's meant to be; above all, *you've felt it through the core of your being.* How else can you know something is really real?

My attention surveyed the surrounding panorama. But this was no small 'I', rather it was the selflessness of the universal Seer guiding the show. All aspects of you must play their part: feelings entrained with interpreting thought, none overriding the other; all working harmoniously as one, like the soft inner ticking of a carefully precisioned Swiss watch.

Then suddenly it all clicked: line of sight connected me to the Tor just as my dream back at the beginning of the year began to play... *"You'll find a high place in Glastonbury not the Tor itself, but a place overlooking the Tor. And there you'll be shown something powerful, a message in lights: its purpose to confirm for you, unequivocally, what's happening at a planetary level."* A slight Sapiens expectation wanted to draw my eyes up into the sky - surely I'd see the lights there? However, the unmistakable Divinicus pull was lower - in line of sight with the Tor, yes, but in the landscape beneath it.

For a moment there was a mild degree of confusion, but this evaporated in an instant, as my human eyes clicked with what was now beginning to take shape in my inner eye: *it was the street lamps that I was drawn to.* Without perfect outer vision - *I'm quite myopic* - the Seer in me finds that, at night especially, unfocussed lights dance together in the most exquisite of ways. I've often wondered why on Earth I should correct this vision? Short sighted myopia, has frequently offered me a priceless key to seeing the entirety of the universe; I've so often been enthralled by it.

And so it was, the lights began to rise, dancing magically off the streets until suddenly I saw it: a V shape, with two long streets of lamplights forming the 'legs' of the V. I say 'legs' with reason: my inner knowing interpreted them as a woman's legs, lying on the ground; and at the place of the apex - *the vagina* - a small foetus like form was emerging. In that moment everything clicked for me: I stood aghast, open-mouthed, until the words flowed unequivocally out... *"My God, it's Gaia, and she's giving birth!"*

It was amazing for all of us. I pointed to the lights, but no interpreting explanation was needed. Those around me saw it instantly too, for they were also attuned to their inner feeling vision: the co-creating weave, connecting us all through a common thread. This was simply divine. We hugged with beaming smiles, warmly, in the frosty night air.

What next? There was nothing else to do: we must go to the site of the birth, the apex of the V, and check out what we might see. So together, happy and smiling, hearts pounding, still with the sense of expectation, we came down off Wearyall Hill onto one of the side roads, linking into the V - *the birthing Gaia.* And as we passed through the small gate onto the road, I could hardly believe my eyes at what we saw next *(except that is, I know that when you're in this depth of multi-dimensionality, all manner of things will materialise physically).* There, parked on the road, next to the gate, was a purple painted land rover. And tied to the front bumper, for some strange reason known only to the owner, was a ridiculously peculiar sight. Something you just couldn't ignore: *it was the leg of a mannequin figure* - a woman no less. *"Yes you're on exactly the right track"* spoke the message, *"You're moving along the leg of a birthing woman".* Unbelievable! Synchronicity was weaving its breathless magic. I know such circumstances may sound strange to the uninitiated, but mysticism like this happens frequently, when you're deep in your energy body; the right triggers spark the activation of 'inner knowing'. They take you way beyond the shallow level of the intellect. No matter how much I experience this, throughout my existence, I will never tire of it.

Next we walked along the 'leg' until we came to the apex of the V, *the vagina,* the site of the birth. Although I know Glastonbury well, for some reason I couldn't anticipate what would be there. So, with the energy of an inquisitive child, I was full of excitement and expectation; not expectation nor need of anything in particular; instead, open to what we might experience. But I knew, beyond a shadow of a doubt, we'd see something poignant, remarkable.

And there it was, the humble Somerset Rural Life Museum, one of those wonderful, ancient buildings, hiding in plain view, that you drive past daily, yet hardly apportion any significance to. It had originally been constructed as a barn: *what better place to give birth to the Christed Child?* Yet again, I was dumbfounded at the interplay. Yet again, the others in the group, Trinity, Lesley and David, were all feeling the sense of divine magic, hanging like stardust in the air.

Guided stepwise by the inner pull, I made my way carefully and softly onto the site, and around the building. There at the back, on the gable end, *was what struck me as a huge 'map',* the size of the gable end itself. Rising up from the ground was a supportive stone buttress, with three steps inwards *"into a Fourth Density"*. Further up, it thinned again, through four more steps, into a *"Fifth Density"*. Above that, was a small angel - *"The Christed Child"*. And at the very top, just under the apex, were three small windows, which translated in my mind as, *"The Holy Trinity"* - the mother of all experience. How utterly amazing. For all those who cared to look up from the sidewalk and feel, it was a map of truly cosmic importance, hiding absolutely in plain view.

Fortunately, we had seen it together. And on that auspicious early morn, there was absolutely no doubt for any of us: *after many years of preparation and processing, Gaia had finally rebirthed into the Fifth Density; a new life was taking shape there, beckoning all who could feel it, to join her in due course.* We were absolutely elated. We'd handed our trust and commitment to the universe, and had not been disappointed. We could now feel an intensified, compelling inner purpose. Like newborns, fresh breath of life had been breathed into us. A new destiny as Divinicus was awaiting.

What would this momentous occasion mean for life here on 3D Earth? How would humanity be unravelled from the matrix and join Gaia in the Fifth Density? As joyful as I now was, these were the questions that were naturally arising next in my mind... *"Be patient my friend, all will come."*

16

Messages in the Movies

"If you truly want to overcome something,
you must first let it succeed.
Suppression overextends itself,
thus exposing its own weakness."

The scene is Nibiru, a class M Planet in a distant star system, about to be destroyed along with all its inhabitants by a super-volcano. Yours is a covert mission to help stabilise the planet, without unduly influencing the evolution of the population.

It is the opening chapter of the Star Trek film "Into Darkness". But as I watched it, something clicked in me. Jaw-dropping, eyes wide open, *"Where on Earth did they get this from?"* I instantly knew, yes, there was a planet called Nibiru, in the Sirius Star system, home to the Annunaki, which was obliterated by the incredible Ascensionary shift of Sirius B 120 million years ago. And although it was hazy, yes, I could recall being a part of a higher dimensional team, working to stabilise the system, long enough that we might assist in the Ascension of the population.

And have you seen the Superman movie "Man of Steel"? Where a distant planet - *home to the character's parents* - is obliterated because the-powers-that-be have drained too much energy from its core. In the film, the shattered inhabitants are left to drift in space until they discover Earth; whereupon, at all costs, they try to take it over to recreate a synthetic replica of their lost home and people. Another fiction? Yes, but it is, for me, a remarkable metaphor of what has been the Annunaki agenda here. Did the film makers have some deeper inspiration?

In fact, there's film after film appearing in the mainstream where you'll catch glimpses - *pieces in the jigsaw* - which can activate and inspire a "Total Recall" of our past life history. Take "Oblivion" for example, where an off-world collectivised consciousness is duping our heroes to assist in the extraction of the remaining resource wealth of the planet. And what about the film "10,000 BC"? In this one, our 'Original Humans' are enslaved to build pyramids for gods: *'who came from the stars'*. My favourite line comes right at the end, *"He is not a God!"*, just as the people rise up and overthrow the dictatorship.

Then there's the raft of superhero movies on the big screen, like "X-men", for example. Where did the ideas for these shape-shifting mutants come from? Yes it may all be pretty tongue in cheek - *an outrageously tall tale* - but nevertheless, there's simply too much inspirational metaphor, not to touch at least some of us in a deeper way. *Yes, in the higher dimensions it is possible to 'fly' at the speed of light; yes, it is possible to shape-shift into different forms, and it is possible to manifest at the speed of thought.*

What's going on, is that we're remembering our heritage, where we came from, often from across the cosmos. The story is bubbling up within the human psyche, so colourful imaginings - *lucid dreams* - are going to continue to appear, with ever greater regularity, as we move forwards through this great shift. The big picture - *the true history* - is still hazy, but that matters not. You don't even have to get the exact detail. The past no longer exists; *but what does exist,* are the influences we carry forwards from it. This is what we, as Homo Sapiens, must now process out. So I've come to love going to the movies, even if it is a part of the matrix, where over-consumption, glitz and glamour is contributing to the negative impact on Mother Earth. I'm reminded that there's truth at the heart of every distortion, and so, if I'm sanctioned to go, *if there's a deeper message and purpose,* I'll go along and enjoy it. Yes, I can recall the place I came from, creating and manifesting miraculous, adventurous and thrilling dreams - *just not at the expense of other sentient life.*

It was in fact the Star Trek movie that catapulted me into a hyper-aware state for several days. Flashbacks, memories and knowings, all whirled around in my consciousness: parts of a kaleidoscope; a mosaic, which piece by piece, fell into place. Many times I would cast the picture out, dissolve it, when my mind simply couldn't accept it. But when it kept reappearing, supported by synchronicities on my journey through the 3D, *and only when it moved something at the core of my being,* then yes, I would accept a strong degree of truth in it. Not that I allowed myself to be fixed or limited by the past. Rather, it would help me release, process, and most importantly of all, *unfold the etheric wings of a new divinity.* Then you absolutely knew, that you were touching some high degree of truth.

It is with this approach in mind, that I share the collated story of Sirius and the Annunaki. Why it has had such an incredible impact on the human journey and our collective karma. But I don't hold this version up as *the truth.* I think it's very close to it, close enough to activate any karmic influences that might be bubbling to the surface for you. And if not, cast it out, until something like the next movie, or shared experience, kicks off something for you. But I suggest you don't get attached to the detail, the facts and figures. To me, they simply don't matter too much, *it's their influences that do.*

So, as the celebrated Zecharia Sitchin has detailed in his translations of the Sumerian tablets, yes there **was** indeed a Nibiru, that **was** home to the Annunaki, and **was** somehow destroyed, which is why they eventually came here. To Zecharia, it was the so-called 'tenth planet' in our solar system. However, I get it differently: it was a planet orbiting Sirius C, which was obliterated in the tumultuous White Dwarf Ascension of Sirius B, some 120 million years ago. Whatever took place there, one thing is for sure, according to many past life regressions I've since assisted with, it was a catastrophic event, which had a shattering impact on the

Annunaki, and other Sirian starsouls who have since found their way here to Earth.

With uncanny similarity to the Star Trek movie, I recall it **was** our purpose to try to stabilise the field of the star system; in order to give time for the population to ascend into a higher paradigm. Thus, they'd be untouched by what was to happen. I recall meeting an incarnated Annunaki soul here on Earth, who could remember me from that time. I was there to bring a message, which had been misinterpreted and misunderstood. It led to them 'ditching karma', accessing the higher paradigm too quickly, switching off to their concealed density, before they'd completely processed their baggage. For them, it created a kind of limbo state: a slow degradation of their proud form over time. Many tears were shed between us, in order to heal this disaster. I carried a deep sense of burden for a long time afterwards. *But it fills my heart with joy, that he is like a brother to me now.*

I have since sat in meditative communion with many starsouls, from other races in the Sirian system. As I helped them regress into their karma; it activated visions and knowings for them. Imagine being in a place where, in one moment, everything seems kind of okay. You already know something big is going to happen (*just like here on Earth right now*), but somehow, you keep persuading yourself everything is 'as normal'. Tomorrow will be just like yesterday. Yes, there are major 'eruptions' going on (*just like on Earth right now*), but surely a planet of this size will handle that?

Then something starts to change, quickly. You don't know what exactly, but you can feel it in every cell of your body - *a phase change of frequency.* You feel decidedly unsure, queasy, nauseous, the very fabric of your reality seems to be unravelling. One moment you feel extremely dense, and the next, extremely light. You keep trying to pretend it's all okay, because the ego likes things safe, secure and cosy.

Then suddenly there's a massive implosion of a nearby sun. Indescribable amounts of light and searing heat are emitted as the electrons suddenly collapse inwards, out of their molecular orbits. Vast waves of energy explode outwards, rapidly, in your direction. As soon as the people get wind of it, there's panic. But it's too late. Your biosphere is obliterated, the air in your lungs suddenly ceases to exist, so you can't breathe anymore. There's a massive implosion and explosion simultaneously. Waves of light signal a sudden quantum phase shift, as your reality begins to bend, warp, and then shatter.

The physical aspect of your body is already compacting down. The unenlightened aspect of your soul, that which is not fully self-realised and consciously penetrating the body, suddenly closes off to the pain, such that you become numb to the lower aspects of yourself. Meanwhile, your energy body is experiencing searing pain; your higher self is propelled into the expansiveness of the higher dimensions. If you've been identifying with the physical, or denying it by kidding yourself you've already ascended, *then it's like being torn apart.*

This is my general observation as to what happened to the Sirian population. Some ascended and made it into the higher dimensions, but these were only a relative handful. Many became bound to the physical remnants of the shattered star system, locked in, by identification with their trauma. Eventually, they'd be swept up into the angelic realms, but it would take time, and other incarnations on other planets *(like Earth)* to truly heal. The Annunaki however, had escaped into the Fourth Density, and now embarked on a different path. They took it upon themselves to start shaping realities. For a higher dimensional soul looking on, it was the worst nightmare, a complete disaster! I can say we carried a great sense of responsibility; the undeniable feeling of having failed in what we set out to achieve. I can't speak for the others, but I assume that many, like me, have carried that burden with them to other locations in the cosmos, just as I have here to Earth. It's a key reason for my incarnation - why I came here.

For the Annunaki, began a deepening departure from the divine.

The events embedded a fear-generated approach of controlling the flow, which life in the 4D greatly facilitated. On their home Nibiru, they had already developed great skill and advanced technology for the manipulation of energy. Especially, what is currently known on Earth as "free energy" - *manifesting from the Zero Point Field* (it's a temporarily moot point I'll return to in due course).

Over a great period of time, their ability to shape and control matter, including other sentient life, escalated with their increasing technical prowess. These 'skills' came to include thought and emotion implantation. Being in the 4D, they were already beyond the boundaries of time and physicality, thus they began to master space travel. It's a 'place' where one can move practically at the speed of thought. All that's needed is a bridge - *a stargate* - some kind of connection to where you want to go to. Essentially this is what takes place when we 'travel astrally' to other cosmic locations in our sleep. It often happens to people without them being fully conscious of it. The Annunaki had mastered how to travel this way whilst still awake. And now these beings - *this collectivised consciousness* - felt cast out, abandoned by God. With their home obliterated, what had they to lose by taking matters into their own hands... *by playing God themselves?*

So the Annunaki became a colonising, warrior race, exploiting other life and resources for their own understandable, but selfish, ends. They colonised other star systems, such as those in Orion's belt, by assimilating the natives – the remnants of which we know today as "the Greys". In their small, prosthetic, synthesized bodies with over-sized heads and almond-shaped eyes, they've been the subject of many a movie. You get a metaphoric glimpse of them in "10,000 BC" as servants to the 'gods'. And who will forget their more cuddly version in the classic "ET"? (*I'll return to the subject of the Greys later*).

Populations were mercilessly exploited by the Annunaki; just as God had seemingly shown no mercy to them. But despite their advanced control of consciousness, and thereby rapidly developing

4D technology, the one thing they really sought continued to evade them: *they wanted to embody, to enjoy the bountiful sense of physical incarnation once more.* And so they experimented. They knew a fundamental universal truth: *they needed a physical vehicle, with a similar frequency to their own souls - for this is how incarnation happens.* Matching polarity draws the two together; by the Law of Attraction, the spirit is drawn into an appropriate vehicle.

To create a vehicle of the right frequency, they needed to master DNA manipulation, a practice which is made much easier from the Fourth Density, where the causal body exists. As its name implies, the causal body *is the cause of material incarnation;* this energy body holds the blueprint for the physical vehicle. If the causal body can be influenced, then the changes are mirrored throughout the physical vehicle itself. That's what DNA is - *a receiver transmitter of genetic coding and shaping information.* How many Hollywood fictions today have been inspired by this reality? Tongue in cheek these films may be, but as we've already discovered, scientists can today influence DNA by the projection of laser light frequency and/or sound, morphing the forming egg cells of creatures from one species to another. *Playing "Frankenstein", is something they'll just have to deal with in their karma!*

So the Annunaki began to experiment, and they travelled far and wide to do so. "Interstellar" travel is not at all hard, when you have no physical body, limited neither by time nor space. A few tens of millions of years later, they happened upon Earth, teeming with life and variation, already a bounteous 'Garden of Eden'. But they weren't the only ones, from the deep cosmos, to have travelled here. They would have to contend with the Draconians: a race originating from the constellation Draco, who had discovered the Earth long before them *(we'll get to their chequered history in due course).* As beautiful as it is for a higher dimensional being to live here, it's also extremely dense and challenging. Perhaps it was this knowing, that H G Wells tuned into, with his classic novel "War of the Worlds", where the alien conquerors were ultimately humbled by the common cold.

For a multi-dimensional being, an appropriate bodily vehicle must be found or *synthesized*. But whether knowingly or not, when a species is introduced to a planet or is seeded, the Devic Consciousness that guides this species must be - *by consent* - woven into the collective eco-system. Here on Earth, it must be rooted into the core fabric by none other than Gaia herself. Visitors are graciously accepted, *but not ones that then go on to misshape the entire fabric of the surface of the Earth.*

Gaia has not sought any kind of retribution, but in various ways, at various times, as the cancer of the Intervention took a virulent hold, then a bubbling frustration would well up, and unleash itself, as a primal scream to rectify the imbalance. Roll on films like "The Day after Tomorrow", "The Day the Earth stood Still", and the big budget disaster movie "2012". It's not that Gaia is in any way vengeful; she has great compassion for all. It's just that there's an upwelling of energy, to re-establish balance; to which the universe responds in the way it knows best - *works in co-creative unison, to unravel injustice and control, bringing ever greater harmony for all sentient life.*

The Annunaki would somehow have to suppress the natural vibration of the Earth; separate her soul from the higher dimensions, and implant energy technologies deep within the core, so as to be able to create a synthetic reality here, and not be ejected. It's a plan, that may understandably sound immensely ambitious; not to mention twisted and distorted! But, with the help of an interspecies alliance *(which I'll come to shortly)*, they've come remarkably close to pulling it off. They created 'the Matrix' - a field of energy, which suppresses not only the people, but the very soul of Gaia herself.

As this all came into my awareness, I couldn't help thinking that Benevolence must have known it would happen; it had occurred in many star systems before. Are we that powerless? As the magnitude of it dawned on me, I felt pretty sickened to my core. Could this not have been prevented?

Yes, it was known beforehand that this Intervention would likely take place, and Benevolence does have its strategies for unwinding it. Here on Earth, perhaps the boldest benevolent involvement yet, was already shaping, even as the Intervention was taking root. Original Humans would form an intricate part of the plan - the 'front line'; an idea to bring the wayward inter-dimensional species back into the light. Essentially, if you truly want to overcome something, you must first let it succeed. Suppression overextends itself, thus exposing its own weakness. By natural processes, the universe will always unwind such control. But yes, where necessary, we can give it a helping hand.

Initially then - *so it appeared* - Benevolence watched from the sidelines, as the opposing entities gathered themselves together, to take over the naturally evolving human story; to own it for themselves, just as they had done elsewhere. Because they had the technological know-how, they would simply use it, without any real concern or remorse for the consequences. Closer hybridisation, adaptation and a 'dumbing down' would ensure that they could suppress souls; overcome them by a form of possession (as we see in the film "The Host"); then essentially create a slave species for their continued consumptive agenda. Above all, they wanted to control reality, and have the full physical, emotional experiences that we humans take so much for granted.

That's why 200,000 years ago, Homo Sapiens suddenly appears, as if out of nowhere. It's why anthropologists can't find the so-called 'missing link'. And around 50-75,000 years ago, you'll see yet another genetic implosion in the human family tree: bones became smaller, thinner and weaker; brains were adapted to reduce the sense of universal interconnectivity; digestive systems were tampered with, to accept the consumption of meat - a way to ensure humanity could go on to populate the Earth. The latter adaptation, was especially important to their agenda of global domination; it meant that they could still populate areas, climates and seasons, where there was only food for grazing animals.

Yet again though, the Intervention was allowed to travel only so far, before the universe's compelling need for re-harmonisation was activated. Once more, the building sense of disorder and out-of-alignment, summoned a reordering force of monumental proportions: this time, the dramatic environmental shifts, at the ending of the last Ice Age, commencing around 12,000 BC. When you research the history, passed down through the ancient texts of indigenous tribes - *from all across the world* - you may get a glimpse of what terrible and devastating times they were: incredible upheaval, powerful storms, comet strikes which blackened skies; erupting volcanoes, earth-crust displacements, and of course, catastrophic floods. All together, they consumed vast swathes of the populated world. Humanity, and with it the Intervention, was all but obliterated *(it's the metaphoric story of "Noah", which made its way onto the big screen early in 2014)*. It was, by all accounts, a powerful 'realignment' *(one which is gathering force once again - which I'll come onto in Chapter 19 "The Great Realignment")*.

Once more, it rekindled the devastating karmic pain of abandonment, that I knew these inter-dimensional entities had felt. No wonder they believed they were experiencing the 'wrath of God'; no wonder they were rebellious and warlike. It was this pain, that I helped reconfront them with, over a period of several years, which included the karmic processes I've shared from my experiences in Berlin and Egypt. I can say that it was with great joy, that I witnessed the healing process of the Annunaki especially: *they'd been confronted with the karmic story of their past; allowed to experience it once more; heal their pain; and experience forgiveness from a higher source.* What's more, they were now able to forgive themselves, as they bathed in a new light of higher divinity. In short, as a collective consciousness, they evolved, ascended and moved on. They were able to let go of their past Annunaki form; they'd reclaimed their stature from their original home in the star system "Anu" (the name by which they call the soul of Sirius C).

Thus, from early 2013, they made it known to me, how important it was to leave this Intervention Consciousness behind; they wanted now to be known simply as "The Anu". It felt entirely applicable:

They'd let go of a part of them that no longer served.

And with that, something fundamentally crucial had happened: *the highest spiritual, controlling layer of the matrix had been unwound. Meaning that the lower threads, were now exposed and, over time, could be unpicked as well.* Whenever something so fundamental happens in the higher field, I always look for its reverberation through the lower densities of the physical realm - *it was only a short while later, that the whistleblower, 'Edward Snowden', appeared on the scene, whose spy scandal revelations have inspired a powerful unravelling and sense of rebellion throughout the physical world.*

As above, so below. This crucial shift in the surrounding energy field, meant that other deeper layers would now become *ripened for the picking.* Next, we would need to work with both the Orions and the Draconians. How would that go I wondered?

Be patient my rebellious friends, for all will come!

17

Dissolving the Pain of Existence

*"The soul will eventually find its way back to the Source;
like a salmon, fighting courageously up the stream,
back to the place of its birth."*

'Life is beautiful', so they say. And indeed in many ways it is: the intricate fragility of the dawn chorus; the power of the bough-breaking gale; sunbeams of nurturing warmth, softly stroking your face. This is the manna of life, which, when you get out of the restriction of the Sapiens mind, you can feel as an intrinsic part of your Divinicus heart.

You have to access the soul in order to sense like this. And so I'd taken myself off to a hilltop woodland, in the heart of South Wales. It was peacefully secluded: a sheltering copse, sitting on the banks of a cool, cleansing lake. I'd come to fast; to do practically nothing, except that is, to penetrate another of the Original Mistakes. This time, it was the "Pain of Existence". Which so attaches people to the need for some kind of outcome in life; anything to take away the boredom, monotony and often misery, in which they find themselves trapped.

No doubt about it, you have to *push the envelope* in some way. A Vipassana Meditation retreat is one powerful approach: sitting in complete stillness for long hours, pushing past the ego's inner resistances, until the light of the divine flows ceaselessly through. But personally, I've always preferred Mother Nature. So I'd fast, sit under a tree, and do absolutely nothing. My 'entertainment' would be to watch the ants scurrying around me, listen to birds singing, or take a naked, ice cold, early morning dip. First though, I'd find a tree and just sit, for at least 36 hours, doing nothing, *not even sleeping.* It's in these still and quiet moments that you encounter The Pain of Existence. And if you truly want to be free, you have to confront it and feel it, for only then can you break through it.

On one such occasion, when the pain of boredom had reached its zenith, I was breaking through and a flow of realisations were unleashed: *there was a time, when the very first souls realised their journey back to the Source, a place of infinite peace and stillness, from where they had originally emerged. Each soul has, interwoven through its very fabric, the memory of this 'Original Condition of Oneness'. So innate is it, so compelling, that no matter how buried and fragmented within the physicality of life, the soul will eventually find its way back to the Source; like a salmon, fighting courageously up the stream, back to the place of its birth. It is this journey, full of hurdles, disconnection and danger, that is the forging of the soul.*

Whilst the phenomenal universe does have a physical Source - *an inter-dimensional centre* - to which life is ascending, this is still only a physical reflection of the true causality of life; which is the infinite potential of Pure Presence, existing in and through all things, literally everywhere. Pure Presence pervades all, within the space between the spaces. It's crystal clear clarity, and when souls have, in the past, touched that space, be they great sages, poets or priests, although described in unique ways, each would instantly recognise the subject the other is defining. There's a knowing, an "aha" moment... *"Yes that's it"*. It's like being in love, you don't have to be told; it's not something you can logic with some kind of formula or prescription - *you just know!* So it is with Pure Presence. You just know.

However, there are many illusions within the internal world of consciousness - *many deceptions and diversionary alley-ways* - to deal with before arriving at this hallowed inner sanctum. There is, for example, the taste of divine bliss: the profoundly joyful connection to the sweetness of life. Bliss is like your favourite bar of chocolate: the more you have, the more you want; and the more you get, the less you can appreciate the subtlety of other experiences.

Bliss, like chocolate, must be an experience you learn to savour, and let go of - *to go beyond.* Otherwise you risk becoming bloated and fat!

Sitting against my very 'ordinary' and earthly tree one day, I came to remember, that bliss is one of those dancing veils on the journey, that you must peel away, to get to the ultimate truth. Eventually, if you're persistent, the veil will fall, and you'll taste the nakedness of life. One fine moment, the bubble of all experience will burst, you'll pierce through the fine outer skin, and drop deep into the endless well, the source of true living: *simultaneously being and not being - Enlightenment.*

It was in the woods this particular time, that I recall accessing the Akashic Records, where the very first souls had achieved this. These 'halls of truth' contain memories: echoes of all that has ever existed, since the universe exploded into reality. The consciousness is contained within the finest ripples of the higher realm. Yet even these are not untouched by the hands of time. All experience is transient; even the records themselves are but reflections, not the truth itself. Here then, is another deceptive diversion on the journey - *the attachment to truth.*

As the great Einstein so eloquently put it, all of physicality is contained within the 'space-time-continuum'. All the multiplicity of form in the universe, is a unified, vast field of consciousness. And there is only one moment - *the moment of now* - through which everything, even the past and the future, are continually morphing and reshaping.

With time on my hands, and no need for any kind of outcome, I came to imagine the known universe as a vast, amorphous jellyfish *(yes really!).* I realised that when it moves, *all of it moves.* So as it's progressing from point A to B to C, then at the mid point B, its shape will contain influences of the past point A, and also essences of the future shape C that it is coming to. For this reason, even though there is no past, present or future - *just one continually reshaping 'now'* - it can feel like movement is happening through linear time; because the mind connects the dots and traces a flow. That's why mystics can look deep into the past and prophets deep into the future; it's why you can leave your house, take a journey on the bus, and arrive at your destination, yet do so all in this one moment of now. Fascinating!

So in these Akashic Records, I witnessed the very first souls arriving experientially back at the Source, and it took me deep into a process. I realised, that although you could drop into the pure stillness of truth, it could only be experienced within some separated form of relativity. There still had to be 'this' and 'that' for me to experience it. 'This' and 'that', whilst creating the duality that renders the very taste of life itself, also means you'll never know absolute stillness as an experience. It's like leaving the busyness of the city, and making your way out into the silent solitude of the desert. I could recall fondly, the first time in this incarnation, I so wanted to switch it all off. Even my beating heart and the rushing echo of silence in my ears, was a distraction to the Void of Presence, that I knew existed tantalisingly beyond all existence.

I'd touched on something, that I believe is the cause of so much suffering for Sapiens. It's why there's the endless not-so-merry-go-round of constantly seeking another distractive experience. It's the reason for so much soft comfort; the cause of depression and anxiety; of Attention Deficit Disorder *(if there is such a thing)* and the like. This then, is The Pain of Existence: it's the knowing that you can never turn the noise off; *that whilst you are an experience as the soul, you'll never touch the infinite peace of the Void as an experience.* When I again confronted this exploration, it took me into a brief state of depression..."*You can never switch the noise of the universe off? That sucks!*"

Then something happened. I accepted the persistence of experience, upon which, I realised that there must be a point on the journey to infinity, where the ripple of experience dwindles so far in the direction of infinite potential, that there is practically no difference between it, and nothing - *no thing*. This 'fudge factor', gives you the taste of the tasteless. In other words, you can have your 'cake' of nothingness and yet 'eat' it too!

Reality is a paradox, an illusion. The Void of Pure Presence, in the background of all things, never went away. *You are that,* and you can know it as a non-experience. But what I'm now speaking of, *is the separated taste of that* - the fudge cake, or the sound of silence that just *crumbles your cookie.* When you can balance these apparently conflicting paradoxes of truth, when you can accept the persistence of the background noise, **and** know yourself as that which is beyond it - *through it* - then you'll burst the bubble of the Pain of Existence.

Until that point however, there are all manner of trials and tribulations keeping souls locked into the pain - *or the bliss (which also, eventually becomes a pain, when you're attached to it).* And I came to find none more deserving of my empathy, than the Greys of Orion.

Have you ever wondered why, when you're doing something that nurtures the soul, suddenly a spurious thought might pop into your mind, about some annoying irritation? How often do you feel, or know a higher truth, only to descend quickly into self-doubt? Why is it that so many people get bored in the stillness of time? Or alternatively, they emotionally flare up, at the seemingly most insignificant of things? *"Oh, it's just an overactive ego,"* many will say. But is it?

I recalled in chapter 6, how in this incarnation, I'd first re-encountered entities morphing through people's fields; shifting from one to the other, activating frustration, anger and emotion. It is these reactive cycles of behaviour that keep people locked into the matrix, bleeding energy, living a subjugated life. And even some awakened people, have reacted by distancing themselves from the problem: living mainly out-of-body, out of the pain, and in some detached, blissful state. Either suppressed or deluded, both are equally effective at denying the authentic experience of the divine being within.

I remember sitting in meditation with a client, facilitating a healing self-realisation, breaking through some destabilising blockages. She was an empath - *able to feel other beings' energy as her own* - a gift many are unable to switch off. They often confuse themselves with the other person's energy they're feeling. Thus, it's a challenge for an empath, to establish their own internal boundaries. For me, as a catalyst, I generally don't experience that kind of problem; I rarely, if ever, lose sense of self. So working with an empath, provides a tremendous opportunity to see yet deeper through the field. And in hers, I'd connected up directly to a group of Greys.

Although mostly I feel, and just plain 'know' the field, this time I could see it too *(such 'clairvoyance' is a precious gift, but we should also realise, it is a 3D interpretation of the 4D, and can sometimes be a distraction from a Divinicus depth of insight into the higher dimensions, which lands as pure knowing)*. So I could see their black, almond-shaped eyes, bulbous heads and gangly bodies - the classic imagery seen on many esoteric websites. At first, the feeling was nauseating - an internal sense of rejection - but I guess curiosity helped me quickly overcome that. As yet, there was no sense of empathy and compassion; *they weren't too keen on me either!*

I could feel a telepathic bridge opening, and an immediate questioning of my experience, which tended to contract my field down - they definitely didn't want me in this space! This is how it works: *they read your field, touch something that might make you feel smaller, and stimulate that limiting thought process.* Interestingly, at the time, I still had an issue around self-doubt. It often walks hand in hand with the interpretation quality of the soul - the "Ray 3" of the Seven Rays (covered in Five Gateways). The Ray 3 is what keeps you connected to authenticity; it's the questioning quality of the soul... *"What's really real?"* The problem comes, when authentic questioning becomes the 'questioner'. Then you create an identity, an ego, which becomes self-limiting.

I was beyond ego at this point, but undergoing a profound shift, finally realising myself as a walk-in, and so my Ray 3 was in over-drive. Nevertheless, I quickly spotted the thread of consciousness they'd started to pull, and the spiral that threatened to contract me downwards. Although it didn't happen, it was a powerful realisation in how they worked, how they limited people's consciousness. Instead, I discovered I could look them square in the eyes, and with the same ray of consciousness, *begin the questioning process within them - why were they doing this?*

As one of them began to open up, and as I expanded with its deeper consciousness in a divinely given, weaving dance, suddenly I could see its journey in the Akashic Records. It was amazing: what a journey - something to behold. Yet it was one that I wouldn't wish on anybody. I saw how a colonising race - *the Annunaki* - had descended upon their star system. Having experienced the obliteration of their home, Nibiru, and still suffering the sense of abandonment by God, the Annunaki were now taking matters very much into their own hands. With eons of energetic experience, and being masters at shaping the field, they became bent on recreating synthetic realities that mirrored the home they had so treasured and lost. *And they needed a slave species to help them do it.*

Stars in Orion's Belt became their next destination. And so they descended upon the innocent, hapless species. I say 'descended', but my knowing is that they 'hung around' in the 4D field, and played a frequency resonance: one that to a soul, tasted like sweet nectar. When you're down in the density, and your soul is not yet fully self-realised, it's easy to be deceived by such deception. So as the Orion souls passed on, ready to join the usual cycle of recovery into the angelic realms, followed by a later, appropriate incarnation, instead, like moths to car headlamps, they were drawn into this honey trap that the Annunaki had set for them.

Just like the combine harvester mercilessly stripping wheat from the chaff, so the Annunaki stripped souls from their designated paths, and instead, inserted them into synthetic energy vehicles; *the gangly ones with black eyes and bulbous heads, that have now become so infamous on esoteric websites.*

This is extremely advanced technology, yes. For the Greys, to be able to morph in and out of various dimensions, seemingly at will, demonstrates an amazing degree of energetic mastery *(on behalf of their Annunaki creators)*. Yet these vehicles are devoid of the ability to experience or express emotion by themselves. And there needed to be a way of keeping the soul in the body; to stop them simply 'taking off the suit' and rejoining the Source. The Annunaki discovered a way - by exploiting the sense of lack and the Pain of Existence. First, they became the father figure to the harvested soul - *"Come sit with me on the right hand of God"*. To a non-self-realised soul, it can be extremely compelling: you're looking for something, that which has been speaking into the very fibre of your soul since the dawning of your existence; something heavenly, divine, compassionate and loving... *It couldn't possibly be the Void of emptiness could it? Of course not!* It can take eons in the journey of the soul to finally realise and accept, that to be with the absolute whole and completeness of 'God', is to be as nothing, and therefore the infinite potential of everything too.

Thus the Orions easily accepted their new 'patron saints', just as any young and naive soul probably would. And it's why they so easily accepted their 'incarnation' into the emotionally devoid energy suits; carefully limited by a distractive vibrational frequency - *like 'white noise'*. The souls were now ensnared, like canaries in cages. Thus, disconnected from the usual cycle of death and rebirth, they'd been sold instead, the endless spinning wheel of purgatory. *Surprised? Why?* You see it today in cities everywhere. How is it, for example, that people can so easily abandon the wonders of Mother Nature, for a treadmill in a gym, senses bombarded and submissively suppressed by video screen 'entertainment'? Yes, I'm sure many who work today in society's ivory towers - *the corporations that have 'mastered' the Earth* - could empathise with the Greys. If they met them face-to-face, and could see into their true nature, *it would be just like looking into a mirror.*

And so the Greys became the worker slaves to the Annunaki. They became the entities that inserted implants into people's fields. As I recalled in chapter nine, implants are energetic 'twists' of energy *- carefully contrived programs, that receive and transmit frequency.* Playing a vibration very similar to your soul-ray-harmonic, they distract the soul from its rightful alignment. Such an implant, inserted close to the third eye for example, will distract from the third eye. Then, because the implant becomes as background white noise, the vibration submerges into one's subconscious. Very quickly, you can no longer feel the third eye, nor the implant that distracts you from it. And since reality is created by what attention is drawn to, you've so easily become disconnected from your sense of true self. Not only that, but like the inquisitive nature of a small child, an unrealised soul will head for the very first glittering attraction to fill the void. No wonder so many kids on Earth these days are lured by computer gaming; it's no surprise how many suffer from "Attention Deficit Disorder". It's the same reason so many empathic women are on anti-depressants; why many men, devoid of true depth of feeling, are lured into cheap-thrill pornography.

This is the human condition on Earth today. Just like the Orions, many have been subjugated into a padded prison cell. Yes, as different as they may physically appear, how ever science-fiction-fantasy it may well seem, Homo Sapiens should easily be able to empathise with his closest cosmic cousins.

So where are the Greys? They're all around you, so blindingly obvious: *they're there with each vacant stare into your smart phone, desperately wanting that incoming text to complete you; they're in your ivory tower, the victimising sense of lack; they lurk in your desperate need to fit in, to be liked, to be accepted; they're fidgeting in the silence, because when you sit for a second in solitude, you just can't accept yourself; they're in that partner, or boss, that you're desperately trying to please; they're there in the cup of coffee, the black tea, the bottle of wine, the comfort food, the pill that you pop to ease the pain of daily life. Take an honest look around you - are they not everywhere?*

So I sat in meditative communion with my empathic client, looking directly through her, and into those sad, blackened eyes. There was no longer any retraction on my part, no longer any blame; they didn't make my skin creep as they had done before. This time, my solar plexus didn't contract down. Instead, as I looked into the void of hell, that this poor being had been assigned to, then it struck me: *I saw the aloneness of a small child simply trying to complete itself.* As I looked through the ether, into the depths of its very soul, all I wanted to do was wrap big, etheric arms tenderly around it, so that together, *we might cry an eternity of tears.* And that's exactly what we did.

To the Grey, this was completely unexpected; it had become so used to the projection, control, and subsequent desolation, that somehow it was eternally consigned to. Instead, through me, it could empathise with the tears, *empathise with itself!* Something started to shift: from the darkest depths, an upwelling to reconnect; even the white noise of its energy suit could no longer suppress it. And, in that tender embrace, I could feel it too. My soul began to vibrate a frequency. And from my crown, a thread of silvery light rose 'heavenward', through the dimensions, back to the Source. A realisation dawned: I was connecting the Grey back to the loving embrace of the divine; eyes widening, the Grey began to physically melt with the joy of homecoming. Telepathically I communicated: *you can take your suit off now; you've found that lost aspect of yourself that completes you; there's no longer any need for the surrogate 'father'.*

Tentatively, the soul of the Grey emerged out from the shadows of its purgatory. Gently, it stepped out into the rising sunlight. Delicately, it accepted its rightful connection back to the Source. Upon which, it rose heavenward; its energy suit fell awkwardly back to the 'floor', like the empty, worn out shell of a chrysalis, as the butterfly unfurls its fragile wings and takes flight. My heart was singing like a choir of angels. No, *there **was** a choir of angels, and my heart sang with them!*

For me, this marked the beginning of the end for the Greys, in their collectivised and limited hive consciousness *(and another crucial layer of the matrix)*. It's an idea, that I believe in due course, will go beneficially 'viral'. And now that the Annunaki 'father', had evolved itself into the 'Anu' and moved on, there will be nothing to stop the Greys from reconnecting to the brother/sisterhood of light. Nothing that is, except Homo Sapiens. You! For you complete each other: you sustain the disempowerment, the victimisation of the matrix; you're what gives it reason... *only as long as you choose to!*

So, does that repressed Pain of Existence serve you any longer? Do the sanitised ivory towers of hell still somehow complete you? Or is there something more? No longer an external goal, an agenda, a 'dead'line that you must fulfil (yes indeed, how dead is that?). Can you let go of the crutch, and find completeness within? Are you ready to challenge and penetrate the pain of the moment, the initial torment of stillness, the completeness of nothing? Because if you are, if you're beginning to hear the dim and distant echo of your subdued soul, then you'll be able to break through and break out, just as my alien friend did that day. And you too will be able to persuade the Grey in you, that it's no longer needed - *that it can take off its energy suit, and reconnect to the Source.* The tide of homecoming is rising: a heavenly swell, which will eventually cleanse all in its path. Like no other, now is the time to liberate yourself, and dissolve this Pain of Existence.

And when you've done that, you'll likely discover there's still one final layer of this limitation to be unwound. For that, you have to go deep into the depths of the physical, and like the vulnerable Hobbit in the Tolkien classic, encounter the 'raptor', dwelling in the heart of the mountain... the *'Wounded Dragon'*.

18

Healing the Wounded Dragon

*"…it's that energy that still gets you up, when all around you is desolate
and broken; it's the fire in your eye,
which just won't helplessly lay down and die."*

In 1979, the space probe 'Voyager' first arrived at Jupiter. It was
only then, that NASA was able to confirm what the psychic, Ingo
Swann, *had already reported in 1973* - that in a similar way to
Saturn: *Jupiter also had rings around it.* When I first came across
this story, I loved it. Not least, because it gets the scientists in a
tizz! By now, I too was flying around the universe, but crucially, *it
was all happening inside myself.* The universe really is within you,
but you have to cleanse and open your inner world to be able to
travel 'astrally'. When you do, you might discover, down in the first
density, your inner 'dragon'. It is for no incidental reason, that the
Buddhist deva, Quan Yin, is sometimes pictured standing serenely
on the back of such a beast, as she 'rides' it.

The first time I fully rediscovered this mystical phenomenon
was during a spiritual workshop I was hosting at a centre near
Glastonbury, which very appropriately had the model of a dragon,
emerging from one wall in the retreat studio. I was guiding the
group deep in meditation, exploring inner child and past life
karmic density. Suddenly, a bridge opened between me and one
of the participants. I could feel instantly what she was feeling: *a
tightness deep down in the abdomen, and then something which
reached up along the spine, coiling around her throat - what I could
only describe as an energetic 'tentacle'.* What happened next, came
much more by intuition, than any premeditated intention.

It was clearly an entity that was possessing her - *nothing unusual;*

as I came to learn, nearly everyone has them hiding unseen within inner recesses. Except this one was really dense, and not nearly as easy to remove as the Annunaki and Greys. It was clearly resistant, and well embedded, trying to oppress and scare me with imagery, but by now, I was well beyond that. And so I found my field expanding naturally to embrace the host, becoming seamlessly as one with her. Then I got the lady to relax; to let go of her fear, to be awesomely okay with what was happening. I enfolded both her and the entity within me, which heightened her sensitivity to the field; she could now feel the tentacle around her throat - *'what do you want to do with it'?* I asked. Calming her nerves, she felt to peel it off - *energetically* - which she did. Upon which, my field suddenly contracted down, naturally - *the entity was now inside me!*

What next? There was a surge of energy up from my dantien. Suddenly, I was riding my 'dragon', up through the dimensions and out into the cosmos. This entity was resistant to recovery within the angelic realms - that was already abundantly clear. And so the next destination was the galactic core, which I could now clearly feel inside myself: *I was literally there.* The entity was dispatched into it, without anger or any kind of malice. But there was the tinge of regret, as it was now being fragmented - *broken down* - in the intense torsional force. So 'who' were these entities? Clearly, somehow, they were related to our inner dragon - *the divine warrior* - arising from one's first density core. I'd known them before, and clearly now was the time to become fully reacquainted; the incident stirred many ancient knowings. It all fell steadily into place.

On Earth, 300 Million years ago, the first Amphibians dragged themselves sluggishly onto land. But as yet, they weren't equipped to explore, and take advantage of, the bounteous wonders that lay open before them. It would take the further evolution of a strong skeleton, powerful muscles, and resilient, scaly skin, for the next evolutionary leap to succeed. The reptiles were that leap. And how they prospered in the treasure trove of life they discovered on dry land. A further 100 million years on, there's a very sudden explosion in Earth's anthropological history: during the Jurassic period, the reptiles 'took off', with all manner of new forms, and a consumptive grossness that has known no equal in the vast history of Gaia *(other than in Homo Sapiens)*. To me, the Dinosaurs ultimately destroyed themselves by their own success; a lesson mankind has not at all heeded. But how is it, that these wildly variant species, suddenly exploded onto the scene?

This was the question that spiked strongly in my consciousness, after my curious entity removing experience. And the answer became almost immediately obvious to me: *they must have had some kind of 'help'*. A while later, whilst back in Berlin, I was sitting in meditation, when 'they' came to me. Initially I wasn't sure who 'they' were. I couldn't see them, but I could definitely feel them, *because their field had a denser feeling than any human*. That's the thing about density, you assume that because you can't see a visual image, they must be light and etheric *(or not there)*. But densities are not the same as dimensions *(although the two often get confused as the same thing)*. Densities are frequencies of existence, and these two beings that had clearly entered my space, were the densest I'd ever encountered *(I might add that you still have to be sensitive to feel them - you still have to be expanded and open to this frequency of the field)*.

A telepathic bridge opened. Apparently they had come to help: *yes, the dinosaur phenomenon on Earth was - in a way - engineered. By us!* They then went on to exchange with me the following (I share it only because it resonated an aspect of knowing within me. As before, I will certainly not share it as 'absolute truth'; rather, something which is accurate enough to activate internal influences that you might be ready to process - like the lady 'host' in my workshop encounter):

> *Draco is a constellation many millions of light-years from Earth. Yet the yearning to evolve, prosper and multiply, is no less strong. The beings that evolved there, imagined an*

extraordinary way of sending their progeny out into the cosmos. One that would require no complex space ships, nor intricate life support systems. Simply bury their DNA inside a rock, a meteor, and send it hurtling off into space - 'intentional panspermia' was their strategy. Thousands, perhaps millions, of these ingenious 'space vessels' were dispatched, with only the lowest success rate necessary.

What selflessness, it occurred to me. Don't even try to send your own body, send instead the building blocks of your progeny, the elementals of life. Then trust that just a few may actually land in an accommodating place, where the consciousness of your DNA could spawn a new species.

These beings are clearly very different from Homo Sapiens. Where we've been separated from one another, *divided to be conquered,* they have instead gathered together as one collective consciousness, one 'hive' mentality. As a race, the Draconian Earth cousins - *what some now call the 'Reptilians'* - although hiding unseen in the physical density, are formidable, highly focussed, highly organised, and highly controlling. They don't blend as such with an environment; rather, as their numbers swell, their aim is to take it over. *But how does life on a far away constellation help the mother species back on Alpha Draconis?* It's a simple truth that Sapiens is only just waking up to: *when you're connected through collective consciousness, distance is simply no object; when you can move beyond the confines of the purely physical, your spirit can be drawn wherever there's such a connection. Master the ability to dispatch your consciousness in this way, and the vastness of space becomes no object at all.*

At some point then, in my knowing, just such a meteor landed on Earth, within Gaia's primordial soup of life, and the DNA contained within it, began to flourish here. When it discovered a life form that might act as an appropriate vehicle, it infused into it, possessed it, and like a parasitic virus, took it over. *That's why the Dinosaurs became so outrageously out-of-alignment with the natural harmony of life here. That's why they spiralled helplessly out of control.* But life has its way of ultimately finding balance again. How poignant then - *how synchronistic* - that just as a rock hurtling from the sky brought this alien life form to Earth, so one would also take it away. Except unfortunately, the comet didn't eliminate the Draconian invaders altogether, only the physical Dinosaur form they had so corrupted. The consciousness of the species itself hung around on Earth, as determined as ever, to infuse into some new life form, and succeed - *thus fulfilling its pathological yearning.*

Roll on a few tens of millions of years later, to the time of Lemuria, as the benevolent seeding of humanity from the hominids was in full swing. It was this species to which this 'raptor consciousness', supported by Draconian entities, now turned its attention; one with the lizard DNA buried deep within its brain; one into which, it could infuse and take over. But as the Annunaki and Orions also found their way to Earth, so the Draconians would have competition. Initially, the two competing sides fought. In ancient Vedic literature, and many spiritual texts, there are stories of *'Gods fighting in the skies',* and indeed there are sites on Earth, where the intense heat of nuclear-type explosions, have caused the formation of diamond-like residue. You don't need some physical 'bomb' to do it. It simply takes a degree of mastery of the energy field.

Eventually, the Draconians departed, leaving their Reptilian cousins behind. And, realising that if they continued to war with each other there'd be no spoils for either, eventually, the Reptilians and the Annunaki *(with Orions in tow)* compromised - *they formed an alliance.* Together, these species would become a formidable opponent to the natural balance of life here. Collectively, they could create synthetic realities, and possess other species in an incredibly sophisticated way. They would distort the flow of knowing, that is the signal of one's soul; supplant it with frequencies of their own, then lure the host species into a synthetic reality. It was all governed by the lustful and desolate need to fill the vacuum, left by their long departed divinity *(from which these species had now been distanced).* Ever watched a mouse going round and round on a spinning wheel? That's the prison the unfortunate Homo Sapiens thus found himself in. With this new slave species mercilessly in tow, the Opposing Consciousness alliance, *would go on to tear the natural eco-systems of this planet apart.*

As challenging as it is to conceive the magnitude of this, nevertheless, I came to realise, most people are simply not 'embodied' enough to realise what's going on in their own fields; their souls are simply not integrated enough through their being. Other energies, other frequencies of consciousness - *like the raptor for example* - are instead infusing through the physical aspect and owning it. Meanwhile, the Annunaki have been influencing the intellect, and the Orions stimulating controlling emotions. So the collective hive-consciousness of these species, has been gaining embodied experience, through the insensitive blind spots that most humans have. These days, I can easily sense when someone is not fully embodied *(most aren't)*, but when I say that to them, they'll often look at me quizzically... *"Of course I'm in my body!"* Yes, the body can still be felt, there's still a consciousness of it, but the soul is not necessarily *infusing through every cell of it.* And since the lower Sapiens mind tends to take various multi-dimensional influences and condense them down into just one stream of reality, then most people don't notice the raptor - *the Wounded Dragon* - acting through their physical density.

It's by this veiled Intervention Alliance, operating through humanity, that a very systematic subjugation of the Earth has now taken place. First, there was the changing and lowering of the Earth's vibrational 'pulse', by playing an ultra low resonant base frequency, anchored by many of the strategically situated megaliths (the Pyramids for example); thus they would suck in, and control, the very consciousness of Gaia. But even that was just the beginning. Roll on a few tens of thousand of years: to Genetically Modified Organisms (GMO), the highly sophisticated attempt at usurping natural plant life; the meat and dairy industry, which enables Homo Sapiens to populate the planet; to Chemtrail Geo-engineering, the maniacal madness of weather control; all clouded by an electrosmog of dislocating gadgetry. Indeed, the take-over is almost complete. From vast experience over millions of years, they wanted to be sure, that their exploitation of the planet and its inhabitants would be comprehensive. All that has so far escaped them, is the complete embodiment of their consciousness into the host species itself, *not by the usual process of reincarnation;* rather, *in a way that they could maintain control.* Possession, to them, has not been enough: it had to be the fully incarnated experience. Thus they would hybridise humanity to accept their own soul frequencies. And working together, patiently over thousands of years, this is what they have done. *Almost!*

So they took the Original Human form, and did some pretty unpleasant things to it. First, they inserted an energetic barrier between the left and right brain. Thus the divine masculine and feminine were separated, the intuitive aspect no longer speaking to the logical. Connection to the Source, and integration as a being, emanates from the soul, but nevertheless, the soul has to speak through some kind of vehicle; if that vehicle has been corrupted, then the end effect is the soul being tampered with too (that is until the soul is 'strong' enough - *self-realised enough* - that such interference cannot inhibit it). This separation also took away humanity's divine gift of telepathic communication - we were no longer able to exchange interconnected feelings, without the use of a clunky language, and a noisy voice box, that take people out of the heart and into the head.

That's exactly where they wanted humanity - *in the head, and so disconnected from his divine heart.* This is where fear was effectively bred into Homo Sapiens. And it meant that he could be conditioned to accept illusionary realities, *painted in the Fourth Density.* Because when an image is created for the mind, if there's no way of testing its authenticity through the processor of an interconnected heart, then it becomes easier to separate a being from the divine flow. Instead, the hapless soul is caused to languish within an eddy current, purposefully created for it. And since lower mind tends to condense multi-dimensional phenomenon down into one stream of experience, those beings are now living just a veiled shadow of the real world.

Next, they weakened the bone and muscle structure, because it would render the species less adapted to the natural environment, and therefore more willing to take on a synthetic reality. Anyone doubting this was done intentionally, rather than by a natural evolutionary process, must ask themselves: 'how is it an evolutionary advantage, for the Hominid stock species (that led to modern humans), to lose at least fifty percent of its strength and robustness, practically overnight?'

A new sense of controlled community would be necessary in order to make this species entirely dependent. And there would have to be a ready supply of food, to support the plan for a burgeoning population, that could eventually go on to take over the world *(the so-called 'New World Order')*. Hence, the adaptation of a digestive system to consume meat; the shortening of the colon, for example, so that the meat would not fester and putrefy *(although, since the average forty year old human still has three or four pounds of undigested, festering meat in his gut, clearly the adaptation was not nearly effective enough!)*. It's also, to my mind, the reason why evolving people frequently face conflicting impulses in moving to a compassionate diet. At a soul level, they'll feel a pull to stop eating meat and dairy; yet, their body still seems to crave it. To me, it's a disharmony that can only truly be resolved by the evolution into the next human form - *into Divinicus.*

Right about now, I imagine many reading will find this all pretty hard to digest. It's a full-on meal! *Where are these Reptilian entities that have supposedly influenced humanity and the Earth? Why can't you see them?* Well that's the point, humanity has been purposefully dumbed down into vibrations so he **can't** see them. You have to purify mind and body *(in similar ways outlined in Five Gateways)* in order to sense the field, to truly know they are there. But then I wouldn't expect anyone to blindly believe me, without direct experience and evidence first. Perhaps then, if you're not feeling the inter-dimensionality of it all, you could instead, *look for the metaphor I'm describing, then consider how the energy of it might be affecting and limiting you?*

Take for example the film "Avatar", where the roles are reversed, with human beings acting through some physical 'puppet'. Or "The Host", where another soul has been superimposed over the original. Consider also Tolkien's classic "The Hobbit", which synchronistically made its way onto the big screen, right at the time this 'raptor energy' within society started to be engaged by Benevolence. For those consciously seeking the deeper meaning of life, the metaphor is so powerful: *the Wounded Dragon - the raptor - is first encountered lurking in a cave, amongst piles of golden treasure that it had plundered; breathing fire, creating a fearful reality, in order to control the population.*

If you ever watch the film, look deeply into the mirror, for you'll see its reflection in every corporation, stacked in the aisles of every supermarket, rampaging across every football pitch. It lurks in the sanitised ivory towers that have governed (and mercilessly raped) our Earth. Adorned in suits and skirts it may be, but the sanitised veils make it no less deadly. Profit and loss, winner and loser, rich and poor, these are the claws of its capitalistic craving. It's the fear and greed mentality of the stock market; the hoarding sense of lack within banking; the fight or flight conditioning of the sports arena; the lustful depreciation of intimate sensuality, emblazoned nakedly across the glossy front cover. It's what separates Sapiens - turning brother against brother, sister against sister. At some level, deep down in the pit of the stomach, it has influenced every man, woman and child on the planet.

What I'm saying, is that this is more a consciousness - a distorted energetic virus - which has seeped into the fabric of the Earth. It has sucked in related, inter-dimensional entities, that now act behind the scenes, in the shadows, but very much controlling the show. The fact that it's not immediately obvious to the eye - without an inquiring consciousness that is - makes it even more effective.

And, I must say, at this challenging point: *it's not all gloom!* There's a very positive side to this energy too, which humanity can reclaim and thereby re-empower himself. In its purest form, it's that consciousness which so often gets the job done, bringing creative beingness to fruition, especially in challenging and demanding circumstances; it smashes through the dogma of the 'can't be done', ripping apart the red tape; it's that energy that still gets you up, when all around you is desolate and broken; it's the fire in your eye, which just won't helplessly lay down and die. Yes, the divine warrior in you, has fuelled some of our greatest achievements, and it can do so again, if we can heal, *within ourselves*, this 'raptor consciousness' - its grossest distortion.

Consider for example, the much lauded 'gut instinct'. The gut literally holds the pack hunting, raptor consciousness - that which is consumed by the need to consume. And just as with its dinosaur patronage, it's become highly effective, generating all manner of ways in which to satisfy its seemingly unquenchable appetite. The gut (in its distorted form) is not just about digesting food, it holds a consciousness that interconnects the aggressive, goal orientated hunters. And it's become highly sophisticated, able to feel the lower flow, through the dense matrix vibration. The gut instinct can quickly rationalise the likely choice made by the 'herd', and what's more, 'head it off at the pass'. This is why it's such a prized possession within society, where profit and loss, predator and prey, oil the wheels of the not-so-merry-go-round *(I would later discover, the healed gut consciousness, is not only deeply compassionate, but full of great knowledge, interrelating with the bounteous wonders of the Earth. It's access to the Earth's field, provides untold wisdom).*

*It was when I'd become fully reacquainted with this final, very dense, physical aspect of the matrix, that the magnitude of it landed solidly in my consciousness. It wasn't so much pennies that were dropping, but big bars of lead! And I can imagine that reading this now, you might feel similarly. So at this stage, it's crucial I remind you of a few vitally important points. First and foremost, we are actors in a drama, a piece of theatre, playing out the Original Mistakes - this one, 'Revelling in Physicality'. No one is to blame, it's simply the universe unravelling itself in the way it knows best. And just as the Earth drew this karma through which to learn, evolve and grow, so did humanity. Secondly, it's only the truth that can truly set you free. You might not agree entirely with my perspective, but even if you agree only in part, knowing an aspect of truth - i.e. what's really going on within society - inspires the path to freedom. Finally, if my sharing invokes any degree of fear, then this fear is already within you. It's only fear that draws this energy, and it's only your fear by which it can control you: these **are not** physical entities, they are etheric, and can only control you by controlling your consciousness. So, if at any time you're in fear, I invite you to go into the heart of it; because when you do so, you'll burst the illusionary bubble of it wide open, then expand outwards, with the greatest joy and liberation possible.*

Fortunately, the angelic realms are also here to help us, not to mention higher dimensional guides, empathic supporters and highly activational catalysts. In doing the spiritual work that I now do, with groups around the world, I am constantly inspired and motivated by the sense of love and enthusiasm that people find within themselves to overcome this Intervention. And I'm frequently reminded by the Team, that both humanity and the planet, hold a very special place in the cosmos: *there's no way either would be left alone, without the deepest love and tangible support!* As I came to discover, sometimes you may feel a little cut off, isolated in it all, especially because of the density of the planet and what's going on here, *but you never are!* It may sometimes feel that way, yes, but that's all a part of our growing process; it's about humanity coming of age, in this vast universe, taking back his sovereignty, becoming self-empowered and, as a soul, *immortal!*

One thing struck me for certain: *if you seek such mastery, if you truly want to accelerate your evolution, way past what might otherwise be possible in a more gentle environment, seek out not the easiest of situations, but the hardest.* Everyone reading has the capacity to do so, otherwise you wouldn't have been drawn to this text, *nor to the situation.* So what kind of things might you need to work on?

It's all about healing your 'Wounded Dragon'. And by that I mean recognising there's an authentic aspect of you, within the 'Revelling in Physicality' distortion: one that you need to align and reclaim. There's a great truth at the core of it, just as with all distortions. This one is about finding the great joy of the physical, the material world, *but without getting lost in it.* And the distortion seems to unduly influence a particular aspect of the soul - *the divine warrior* - a feature that both men and women carry. So in short, the way to best heal this aspect of humanity, is to enjoy the physical in its very fullest, but most important of all, *to find aligned behaviours within it; behaviours that revel in the joy of life, but not at the expense of other sentient beings.*

In so doing, we send out a frequency of realignment. Everything is connected by threads of consciousness, which we are either being influenced by, or are influencing. Right now, hiding surreptitiously in the shadows of inter-dimensionality, the Reptilians have been pulling on humanity's lower base frequencies for thousands of years. The time has come to reclaim your power!

So let's take a look at our physicality in sport, for example. As I sometimes consider Chris' life, I recall many hours pulling on a rowing blade, pumping iron in the gym, and conditioning the body in martial arts. Much of it was fuelled by the raptor's need to compete and succeed *(at the expense of another)*. As I looked deeply through the cells of this newly acquired body, I could feel how unity consciousness had been literally squeezed out of it, like the threads of high tensile steel, twisted and contracted. That's what so often happens when we 'train' the body - *the risk is we desensitise it* - creating blind spots within, literally shutting out higher consciousness. As I got used to physicality once more, I'd frequently wake up in the morning, finding my body twisted in some kind of residual tightness and pain of the past - *it had to be unwound*. And so, by bringing conscious awareness into movement, surrendering and softening into the muscles, I revitalised these once deadened areas. That's why healing practices like yoga and tai chi can be so invaluable. They're not the only ways though. Personally I love feeling the fullness of the physical body, with the skin sweating and heart pounding, as I fast-walk through the countryside. Press-ups, dips and sit-ups yes, but now, I do so consciously, feeling fully, and never going beyond what feels aligned for my body. It is of course, all about staying present, and this too helps immeasurably to heal the Wounded Dragon, *unwinding the clutch of the distorted raptor.*

Another area where it's easy to get lost in the physical, is of course food *(never have so many books been written!)*. During my journey of conscious immersion into incarnation once more, the divine has encouraged me to move progressively back to a higher pranic, plant-based diet - *that of the Original Humans.* I recall a particular cleansing fast, using bentonite clay to remove what's known as 'mucoid plaque' - a festering mess of detritus, left in the colon after years of meat and dairy consumption. As the toxin was cleansed from my body, it was as though the very claws of the matrix - *of the raptor* - were being released from my colon. It came with an incredible sense of lightness, and a heightened depth of sensitivity to the field. But I also discovered that I shouldn't deny this now-healing Dragon either, because it languishes in the depths of our DNA. So I sought out more healthy forms of protein, and the denser vegan foods, like beans, nuts, grains and pulses. Especially when I'd been highly active, and processing tonnes of energy, I came to know that I'd always need to look after this now-healing Dragon: I'd use placating, comforting and filling foods; the sugars too, I don't deny those, I've just found more healthy versions of them.

In considering the sweetness of life, we must also reclaim our sovereignty within sexual intimacy. With thinly veiled pornography bandied around on every glossy magazine shelf, it's hardly a surprise that there'd be distortions, denials and taboos to break through. And total abstinence is not going to help heal this consciousness either. Coming fully into the physical body, and sharing with another in this most sensual of ways, is for me, an utterly sublime path to divine union. To be bathing in the rosy hue of sensuality, senses tingling, juices flowing, is to be tasting the manna of physical life itself, *the very nectar of the flower.* But you must also know the illusion in it: so, to be totally, *one hundred percent,* fervently within the passion, *but not at all lost in it;* on the point of being lost, yes, *but not lost;* fulfilling oneself, yes, *but not selfish;* enjoying the passionate physicality of the divine masculine, yes, *but never manipulative.* As with the varied tantric practices that have sprung up over the years, you find there's **more** joy to be had by managing one's energies **not less** (not least because the experience lasts longer!). And, contrary to what some tantric practices advocate, I've found that to release one's sexual juices is no hindrance to divine union either. For me, it's all about the energy - *the consciousness.* So, on the moment of release, as the sexual juices blend and flow together, I'm bringing my attention into the energy, rising it up through my spine, around my body and embracing my partner in it too. Just like a heavenly rocket, the energy shoots you up into the crown, and thus the higher dimensions, where you connect intimately with your Twin Flame. It's absolute bliss!

In my view, life wouldn't be worth living without emotion, passion, courage, commitment, bravery and will. I feel to be immersed completely in the fullness of these experiences too. These are also the feelings of the Dragon, which have inspired some of mankind's greatest achievements. So to deny and suppress these important aspects of the oneself, is not only going to be defeating from an evolutionary point of view, it's also going to be emasculating as a being. Yes I agree, it's not right to lose oneself in anger, as the raptor has done, with projection onto other sentient beings. We must find ways to channel this energy into positive, emotive and creative action - *a sure way to heal it*. I've found that, in the very moment where you might get angry or excessively virile and 'blow your top', if you can instead, contain the energy and channel it into some form of physical, emotive and aligned expression - *like vibrant sport for example* - then you don't deny crucial aspects of you. You're stirring up the bed of the stream yes, but in so doing, you're finding and reclaiming lost nuggets of soul gold buried there. What's more, when you do this, you're giving any Reptilian entity that might be dwelling in your field, a reason to heal and evolve as well. And this is vital to the healing of humanity. You're saying to it... *"If I can do this, then so can you."*

To me, as I would subsequently experience this as a crucial purpose of the Original Human, and now Divinicus: to heal the raptor consciousness by realigning our behaviour; not to fight it; but neither to give in to it.

> *It's having the will to stay connected, harness and manage this energy within you. And to do so in truth - in a way that encourages the wayward Reptilian, connecting to you through the field, to do likewise.*

I came to remember this is the amazing opportunity and mission for humanity: *that we have the capacity to heal the Reptilian, by working with the raptor consciousness within ourselves.* To point the finger, blame and judge, will only cause the entities to fight back and thereby persist. We must now find the biggest hearts of forgiveness, and thereby solve one of the universe's most fundamental problems - *Revelling in Physicality* - one of the Original Mistakes.

*In my knowing, which the Team have clearly confirmed...
The indwelling raptor consciousness **will** be unwound; the
Earth **will** be reclaimed from this unjust and unbalanced
Intervention. Those entities that surrender to the flow, **can**
be recovered and relocated elsewhere in the cosmos, to
continue their evolutionary journey. But those resisting, will
likely be fragmented through the core of the galaxy...*

This is no negotiation.

You and I can each help by realigning this 'raptor distortion', first
within ourselves, and then rippling that realigned incentive out
into the wider world. The Reptilian entities are going to feel pretty
insecure as their distorted reality is stripped away from them. There
will be many last ditch attempts at control, many final lashes of the
tail. We'll see, no doubt, their human counterparts also trying to
cling on tooth and nail - *those secret societies that have willingly
acted as their puppet avatars.* However, as I said earlier in chapter
11, their ultimate spiritual power - *the distorted Lucifer* - is gone,
as are the previously resistant Annunaki. So finally, after millions
of years of controlling Intervention, *the Reptilian entities will be
completely cleansed from the Earth.*

This time though, it will not be by some singular event, such
as a meteor striking the planet, a super-volcano exploding, or
some great flood. The cancerous raptor consciousness has taken
such a deep-rooted, virulent hold of humanity and the Earth, that
something much more comprehensive is now gathering strength
through the field. It is greatly needed to correct the imbalance:
to cleanse, and find equitable harmony once more. I'm certain
humanity will be given time, yes; but the mirrors to this veiled
aspect of himself, must now get steadily clearer and stronger; such
that he can be healed, and crucially, so that the planet can be saved.

This time, it will take a "Great Realignment".

19

The Great Realignment

*"The Intervention that has wound Sapiens into it,
has infected the planet with unsustainable consumerism,
bringing it to the point of destruction. Thus the realigning force
would need to cleanse the surface of the Earth in its entirety."*

A heart-felt pull had drawn me out into the deserts of Arizona. I'd always resonated with the message of the Hopi Elders. They'd spoken of "The Great Purification", as they'd termed it. What exactly did that mean? As my shaman friend, Ken, and I approached the ancient Hopi settlement of Oraibi, the oldest settlement in America, it was already dusk. We'd driven several hours across wide open plains, a vast untouched landscape, punctuated now and again by the most majestic of mountains. The landscape was speaking to us. As the clouds danced across the heavens, the feeling was other-worldly, transcendent, *Ascensionary.*

We made first for the Hopi Prophecy Stone, a depiction of how the elders thought mankind's tenure here on Earth was going. The carving depicts (amongst other things), two possible paths for mankind: one, that of ever increasing technology, leading to sudden oblivion; the other, natural realignment with nature, leading to a renewed life in a renewed world. They spoke of nine signs that would signal the beginning of the Great Purification, the final one being the return of the Blue Star Kachina (a kachina is what I would interpret as a 'deva' - a cosmic soul that unites a particular species or group consciousness). Some believe all nine signs have already been fulfilled; the ninth being the falling to Earth of the space station Skylab in 1979, which looked blue as it came into the atmosphere.

When I heard about this incident, I instantly felt something twinge strongly inside: a deeper meaning, a deeper synchronous message. What spoke to me was 'the falling of the skies'. 'What did that mean?' I wondered. I was reminded of the images I'd seen during my car-crash-incarnation. I sensed some major reconfiguration in our atmosphere taking place, which would radically change the biosphere of our planet. The Hopi spoke of fire. Perhaps it would be 'fire from the sky?' At the time I didn't know, but I knew that if it was important, I'd be shown exactly what it meant, somewhere further down the path.

That night, as we left the stone, for some particular reason we took the wrong dirt track, ending up lost in the middle of the desert, forced to retrace our steps. I was reminded that no mistake is ever a mistake, unless you fail to learn by it. And the universe will sometimes play games with you, because it 'wants' you to step beyond the ego to get some important message or other. So our diverted wanderings in the darkness, through the desert, meant that in exactly the right place, at exactly the right time, a meteor - *with shades of blue in it* - streaked across the night sky and came down directly in front of us, way off in the distance. It was one of those divine messages that quickens your pulse and races your breathing. You don't debate truth as some intellectual pontification: I find this the least inspiring trait of Sapiens. When the universe grabs you by the balls however, and asks: *"are you getting this one?"*, you certainly don't want to deaden your feelings with some mind-led debate. And just to be certain I was reading clearly, my trip to the States concluded in Santa Monica, meditating on the beach at dawn, my attention drawn to a brightly lit, morphing ferris wheel. The very last image in the sequence was a blue star. No, I didn't need to engage in some tiresome debate with the intellect, this was the mother tongue of the universe speaking loud and clear; there was not one shred of doubt in my being...

All nine signs were already complete and
The Great Purification had begun.

To the Hopi, there was no debate either. They saw that mankind had moved so desperately out of alignment with the natural balance on Earth, that life itself would restore harmony once more. I was reminded, yet again, that all life is connected by threads of consciousness: *the unity aspect yearning to flow back to the Source.* And so, when you put a dam in the stream, the flow of Unity Consciousness will build up behind it. And what's more: *the higher you build your dam, the stronger the force against it becomes, until nothing can withstand its realigning pressure.* The only question to be answered was... 'What would that look like?' The Elders spoke of a world conflict, with 'America being destroyed by fire and radioactivity'. Only those who'd discovered their spirituality would survive... for this 'would be a spiritual conflict with material matters'.

Firstly, I should say I don't believe in prophecy, because the universe is continually morphing and reshaping - just like the vast, metaphoric jelly-fish I mentioned. As swings in mood, emotion and thought take hold, so the future is reshaped as we move into it. Nothing is fixed. *However, when a body of energy is moving in a particular direction, like lemmings towards the cliff edge, there comes a point, where practically nothing is going to change their direction - it's clear they're going to topple over the cliff.* It's not so much that astute spiritual beings can accurately prophesy the future, it's more that they're able to accurately read the truth **of this moment.** And, being able to do so, they can call more or less where the flow is heading. To me, that's what the Hopi Elders were able to do.

What they'd seen, is what many spiritual people see across the planet today: *that due to some unseen Intervention through the field, life has become totally out of balance with the natural harmony.* An eddy current of false identification with the physicality of life has been created, in which humanity is trapped. It's not mankind's fault. He's simply playing out the karma of the Original Mistakes, manifested as an Opposing Consciousness, which has disconnected from the flow, and has been fervently trying to control life through humanity. It can't last. It won't last. *It's already kicked the Earth and her eco-systems into an irreversible sequence of events, that cannot now be turned back.* On countless occasions, where I've encountered the Intervention at first hand, I've held and radiated a frequency - *an energetic message* - piercing right into its very heart...

> *Everything is influenced by the flow of unity consciousness in a particular direction - to ever higher vibrations of interconnectivity, sense of love and harmony. So strong is this movement, that ultimately nothing can withstand its unifying force. Even the strongest concrete building will ultimately topple. Unity consciousness is that force which destabilises outdated, inequitable systems, so that more evolved ones can come together with greater harmony. It's a force, which can destabilise the very structure of the atom, causing it to break down, as happened on Sirius B, 120 million years ago. In that case, it caused a sudden implosion of the material, and an explosion of light, as the unity consciousness buried within materiality released itself. Such was the incredible force of its Ascension. And the energies at work on the Earth right now, are of no lesser strength.*

Mother Earth has cleansed herself five times in her history - *five mass extinctions* - where the natural harmony and balance of the planet has, for some reason, moved out of alignment. It's not that Gaia is angry, she is not vengeful as some would have it. She is a highly evolved light being, deeply compassionate for all life in her fold. However, when such a sentient soul experiences imbalance and injustice, a yearning to correct the imbalance is established within that being. *And remember, she is a devic soul, consciously connected across the vast cosmos. She is, in no way, helpless and alone.*

Do you not feel that very same need for realignment, when

you witness harmless creatures being mercilessly brutalised and trampled by the matrix? Do you not feel it in the supermarket, with its packaging and preservatives, its chemicals and GMOs? Do you not feel it on the motorways, in the airports and train stations? What about the towns and cities, that have so plastered themselves on top of the sentient creatures that once existed there? I put it to you: that the higher self in each person is yearning - *practically praying* - for truth and realignment to now happen, even if the ego is still resisting.

Some will no doubt say... *"It's all okay, Gaia can sustain us. All we have to do is get rid of the capitalistic powers-that-be, reduce our consumption from the 1.5 Earth's resources we're currently consuming, and divide what she can comfortably provide fairly amongst all humans. Advanced 'free energy' and the like will save the day."* I can't believe that anyone who thinks this way, has actually tended an organic garden, doing so consciously; a garden that cares equitably for the slugs and the bugs, the aphids and the ants. Now expand that compassionate principle across the entire surface of the Earth - my point being: *that all creatures require their natural habitat and space too.* Do they not have a voice? Are they not also deserving of harmonious living? I can tell you for sure, that Gaia and the higher realms of Benevolence think so.

Indeed the Earth began as a balanced and harmonious eco-system, acting as one, serving all life upon it. If one life form, for some reason out-reached itself, a 'trip switch' would be thrown; cleansing would happen, and balance restored. Except in this case, where fuelled by the inter-dimensional Opposing Consciousness, humanity has stamped its mark of resistance across the depth and breadth of the planet. In my view, if the current population were to find balanced harmony with all life, we would need not one Earth, **but ten!** And as for 'free energy', there is simply no such thing. Yes, energy can be summoned from the zero point field, but the Earth is a self-contained system: meaning that whenever extra energy is applied **into the system,** all life will be affected.

You could imagine it this way:

You're living on the shores of a lake. Everyday you have to walk around the lake to gather food from the other side; it's a pretty long and tiring journey - yet it does keep you fit, and the scenery is breathtaking, so it's not too much of a chore. Then one day, an idea dawns to make a boat and oars from a fallen tree, which halves the journey to the other side. As you happily paddle your boat across this once perfectly still lake, the ripples stir up the other sentient life in it, but only very marginally, in a way that is not harmful. And now other people in your village have the same idea, and they too build boats that they may cross to the other side.

Roll on a few thousand years later, whereupon, your descendants have discovered how to power their boats with outboard motors and petrol, which spares the tiresome job of paddling. Now the energy applied into the lake, is exponentially increasing as the population of the village rapidly grows; it's decimating the once harmonious life living in the lake.

Such is the imbalance now on Earth; such is the sense of injustice; and so, such is the sense of yearning for correction. Some will say that free energy, manifested from the zero point field and other clean energies, will mean that other life doesn't have to suffer. As seductive as that may sound, it's also pretty naive. Because firstly, it does nothing to diminish the energy you apply **into** the system when you consume it. Secondly, I ask what would it do to the size of the global population, which is already expanding at an exponential rate? What would that burgeoning population do with the old oil-based machines? Simply cast them aside? Where would the resources come from to build the clean energy devices? It is these inconvenient questions that cannot be swept under the rug. The strong likelihood is, that so called 'free energy', would only *increase* the back-breaking burden on Gaia.

The evidence is there for all to see. Back in the early 1800's, just before the beginning of the Industrial Revolution, the human population of Earth stood at around 900 million. Despite the mis-shaping of some areas for agriculture, it was a way of life that was reasonably in balance with Nature, and one which the Earth could fairly comfortably withstand. The discovery of coal and steam power changed everything, practically overnight. Suddenly, humanity's exploitation and wanton destruction of the Earth took off in a big way. As a result, the population literally exploded off the chart, and with that, our ability to shape, change, control and plunder the Earth skyrocketed. Take a look at this graph below, from Wikipedia, showing the growth of world population over the last twelve thousand years. Personally, I find it literally jaw-dropping...

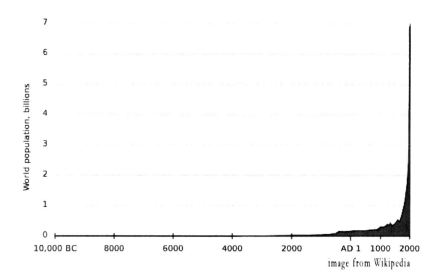

image from Wikipedia

What will the introduction of new, advanced technologies do to that chart? I'd say it should be absolutely obvious to all - without some major correction, the population can only increase. And so to me, it was quickly becoming clear - *the solution now has to be much more radical.* I hasten to add, not one controlled or manipulated in some unnatural way by humanity. We have to allow the natural guidance of life to shape the path for us. Although I've worked with alternative possibilities, and dissolved the inconvenient truth many times, hoping something else would materialise, I found myself arriving at an inescapable conclusion:

> *The Intervention that has created the hybridised - totally dependent - Sapiens form, has infected the planet with the raptor consciousness of unsustainable consumerism, bringing it to the point of destruction. This consciousness has no place on the newly forming Fifth Density Earth, and cannot be allowed to interfere with the creation of a balanced harmony for all life there. Thus the realigning force would need to cleanse the surface of the Earth in its entirety.*

My heart was heavy: *is that really the only viable solution?* I processed it through my consciousness for some considerable time, going backwards and forwards through other possibilities. But the realigning jigsaw pieces all kept landing in the same places. Ultimately, I was consoled by the vision of a renewed Earth - *in a higher vibrational consciousness* - a new, pristine 'Golden Age'. And that ultimately, a new humanity - *Divinicus* - would walk the surface once more, only this time, with no Intervention, and a much softer footprint. To me, as challenging as the realisation of this Great Realignment was to embrace, that had to be worth it.

And at times, I still wondered, 'might there be another way? At this stage, I still found it immensely difficult to accept this as my truth. So the universe kept taking me in hand. The pull *(the realigning one, now flowing strongly),* guided me to seek out evidence on the internet of what's actually **already** taking place. What I discovered, was that under usual background conditions, animal extinction happens at about the rate of 10 to 100 species a year (estimated from geological readings). Today however, we are witnessing the unprecedented extinction of at least 100 species per day. Yes, that's **per day!** That's according to reputable sources which you can easily check. And then, I was drawn to a deeply poignant Greenpeace quote: '*4.6 billion years of the Earth's history, scaled down to 46 years, would see humanity emerging in only the final 4 hours, the last minute of which, representing the Industrial Revolution. Since when, over half of the planet's trees have been destroyed*'. Does that not shock you to your core as it did me? Do you sense the stark-staring reality of it? Sometimes life does this; it dumps you unceremoniously right onto the blade edge of existence....

"Here, deal with that. Deny it if you dare!"

It's like the current 'debate' about global warming. Elements of humanity, no doubt influenced and fuelled by the ever-present Opposing Consciousness, have turned the emphasis of the truth into some scientific debate; about whether the climate is heating, cooling or whether there's less ice in total or more. Frankly, they'll still be debating even when the cows stop coming home! Let's be clear: *this is about the wholesale destruction of our biosphere, happening now, in front of our eyes.*

Each previous mass extinction has been preceded by ocean acidification and the rapid dying off of ocean life. That's exactly what we're witnessing now - according to Greenpeace, ocean acidification is happening at it's fastest rate for over 300 million years. And exactly where is that acidification coming from? It doesn't take the brains of an Einstein to figure that one out!

Of course the Opposing Consciousness in the background does not care - it's trying to take control of the Earth to create its own synthetic reality. Hence, like a parasitic virus, it will invade, twist and usurp many of the 'clean energy' and eco-friendly movements, if that means its hybrid human progeny can continue to thrive. But this time, they've underestimated the treasured place that Earth has in the cosmos, and the collective yearning to reclaim both it, and humanity.

So the Soul of the Earth, and all other sentient creatures, are yearning for change - *to dispense with the raptor consciousness of dog-eat-dog* and move into a higher vibration. Gaia will now dispel the outdated karmic consciousness of 'predator and prey', 'fight or flight', and so-called 'survival of the fittest'...

> *This must now be the survival of those that can live instead, within a realm of co-creative harmony, which supports all life, not exploits at the suffering expense of another.*

This soul-yearning is the very compulsion that drives the cogs of the cosmic realigning wheels. Life must respond. In the case of the dinosaurs, a beacon of light emitted a clarion call out into the cosmos to correct the imbalance. It was answered by the comet, that ended their inglorious reign.

> *Don't misunderstand me, I'm not saying the comet was conscious! I'm saying that all life is interconnected, and so when the yearning for correction is aligned with the natural flow, events shape to restore balance once more.*

This time though, I sensed the realignment would be very different. Gaia has evolved, and so her answer to the problem would likely be much more sophisticated. She'd certainly want to allow time and space for her children to realign, for as many as possible to come back into the universal fold. *'How would that work; what would it look like?'* I wondered.

It was now 2013, and Gaia had already ascended: *specifically, she'd shifted her centre of consciousness into the Fifth Density.* Once more, my inner journeying brought me back to the spectacular Olympic opening ceremony of the previous year: the Five Golden Rings - *the Five Gateways* - in blazing light, hoisted above the stadium for millions to witness. People around the world, were glued to their TV screens, as the loving heart of Gaia was decimated by the industrial 'satanic mills'. But then, in blinding lights, all were shown the pathway into the higher paradigm - *even if, at that stage, many weren't able to understand.* What theatre and spectacle! I shall remember it all the days of my life, such was the artistic connection to the underlying story, that the ceremony's creators had somehow accessed. It was nothing short of miraculous.

*And there was an even greater significance that many have not yet read. It's an even more poignant message, and crucially important indicator, that is being covered up by the mainstream. It is one that in due course, I believe will affect all sentient life on the planet, **including every single man, woman and child**.*

The Hopi spoke of the Earth cleansing by 'fire and radioactivity', that only spiritual people would survive the Great Purification. Back in 2011, on the 11th of March, an earthquake in the Pacific Basin launched a terrifying Tsunami, that ripped apart the Daiichi Nuclear Plant at Fukushima. I can recall it very well: our Five Gateways Documentary about our 'Journey of Ascension', was due to be released, **on that very day.** But out of respect for those who suffered in the initial catastrophe, we held back the release of the film until a week later. Within the small team that made the film, we could very much feel a greater significance of the moment, yet none of us could fully appreciate the enormity of what was beginning to take place. But now, as the pieces of this complex jigsaw were swirling and landing around me, the significance of this powerful synchronicity dawned...

Just as the sinking of the Titanic was a prophetic warning, signalling the impending disaster of the Industrial Revolution, so The Fukushima Tsunami marked the beginning of what the Hopi called "The Great Purification", and what I am now given to call... "The Great Realignment."

It was certain to me, that this Great Realignment had begun; an inevitable sequence of events has been set into action; various 'trip-switches' that, over time, would radically change the surface of Third Density Earth.

At that point, it became vitally important for me to understand, what in outline, might actually take place. We could never know the detail of each twist and turn - *of each person's fate* - but in knowing the general process of this realignment, more people might be inspired, and better prepared, to deal with the consequences. *Crucially, they might be more prepared to let go of the collapsing old-world values and embrace the spiritual path.* As I began to share my realisations with people, yes, just like me, they found it tough to take in at first. But I remind them: that all life is transient; that you were never meant to live in one form eternally, despite society continuing to limit people by not providing the empowerment of passing on with grace and dignity. Passing on is not sad. Quite the opposite. It can be the most expanding, liberating experience of your life; where you, *the soul,* are released from the density. Spending a lifetime limited by fear is the real tragedy. The Divinicus in your heart, knows its eternal place in the universe.

So I continued to reflect on how it might all fall into place, calling on the knowledge and insight that I'd had prior to my incarnation, before the density of this place had temporarily stripped it from me. As ever, the Team would not tell me exactly, but they were always on hand to guide me to signs and synchronicity - *'how do you feel about that?'* The Hollywood film, "2012", came to mind, with its galactic alignments, pole shifts, earthquakes, earth crust displacements, supervolcanoes and solar storms all delivered with the final, earth-cleansing flood. For those thinking *'it's all just Hollywood glitz and glamour',* the point is: many of these kinds of events actually took place at the end of last Ice Age, as I've previously described. And it culminated with an almighty flood; the difference being, it didn't all take place in a few days *(of course that wouldn't make for such a dramatic movie!).*

'What if though, that which had been predicted in 2012, wasn't wrong in its entirety, just wrong in its timing and completion?' This was the thought that prevailed upon me next. The swirling stream of consciousness, took me once more back to my car-crash-incarnation, and the visions which accompanied it. Despite being at times desperately confusing, one thing was certain right from the outset: *that my incarnation coincided with events of monumental proportions now taking shape on the Earth.* Gaia, and all benevolent life on the planet, have been emitting a signal out into the cosmos, yearning for the imbalance to be corrected, to ascend and move on to a higher harmony of existence. Many souls have responded to the call. I was one of them. And I came in with a vision, a message to share with everyone. A part of it was first delivered by Chris, when Five Gateways was first released...

"We stand on the brink of a miraculous new evolution for mankind. A higher vibrational reality is beckoning us, founded on unconditional love for all life and synchronistic co-creativity; it is a 'heaven' which exists here and now all around us. In this new paradigm, we are completely at one with each other and all life. There is no killing, manipulation, or exploitation of ANY sentient life form or natural resource. All is shared and experienced in harmony without fear. There is absolute trust in our at-one-ment with the divine. Indeed we experience ourselves AS THE DIVINE, not separate from it. Our living purpose is self-realisation and spiritual enrichment.

The new paradigm is already unfolding all around us, but it is difficult to see, taste and feel, as the old world values crumble and collapse. All life and all structure is formed from universal life energy - from pure consciousness. Nothing is stationary, the underlying fabric from which all life is woven, is naturally evolving to ever higher states of harmony and at-one-ment. It is a river of life, flowing ceaselessly through every single moment and nothing can resist its eternal flow. Anything that is of lower vibration, lower harmony, anything that sustains inequity and the selfish exploitation of life, will over time, literally fall apart.

That is what is happening to our society right now. To many, it is an inequitable and unjust system based on exploitation, fear and greed. It is one that has unceremoniously shunted our existence out of harmony with our planetary system and our universe as a whole. Industrial consumerism, the supposed 'virtuous' building block upon which the very fabric of our society has been founded, is now tumbling. It has become an insatiable beast that has been raping Mother Earth in this realm, stripping her bare of natural resources to fix humanity's ever burgeoning addictions. We have built a society on false promises and written countless blank cheques which can no longer be cashed. We have founded our lives on sand, and the tide is now fast coming in.

As this turbulent transition takes place, we are each being invited to join the new paradigm; we each have a ticket for that journey. To get on board, we have to go within, peel away our attachments to the material world, process out our fear-based thinking and dissolve distorted behaviour patterns that limit us. It is these that constrict and confine us in the lower level of consciousness. We are being invited to separate out the authentic characteristics of our soul, from the conditioned beliefs, illusionary needs and false agendas that have been programmed within us. We have to let this darkened veil fall from our eyes so that the new world can unfold into view.

So in this eleventh hour, we are each being presented with a choice: either we continue to buy into the collapsing fear-based mentality of division and struggle, or we step into the heart and reconnect with our divine birthright. Benevolent Consciousness is drawing ever closer to help those prepared to listen. We are being provided with a route map through the inner landscape. The map guides us through Five Gateways of consciousness, leading to our Enlightenment and Ascension into the higher paradigm. It is a process that has been followed by spiritual masters throughout the ages and has the power to unite evolving people everywhere.

We each follow a unique pathway as we ascend the spiritual mountain, but those who have climbed before us, report similar experiences, challenges and opportunities as we pass key 'altitudes' en route to the summit. The map is a gift to humanity in these profound times of great change. It offers the priceless opportunity to come to know ourselves experientially as what we truly are - the "Seer" - an eternal presence through all creation. In so doing, we move back into harmony with the natural flow of the universe and unfold the magical lives we were born to live."

Of course, this part of the message deals with the imperative for human spiritual evolution as the Great Realignment kicks in, and the old fear-based reality falls apart. But it isn't specific about where exactly this new paradigm will be; which is vitally important, because many speak of it unfolding here on 3D Earth.

So is this higher vibrational frequency here all around us? What will happen to the Physical Earth and those not yet ready to ascend through their karma?

Furthermore, many people I began sharing with, wished for some insight as to how it might unfold; and especially, how are people supposed to live, as the old reality is shattering all around them? Neither does the view specifically deal with those who are resistant to the evolutionary process, who refuse to acknowledge the warnings; what about the powers-that-be in society, who still have some dwindling degree of resource and control? For they will, no doubt, still try to manipulate the 'Titanic' as she sinks. All these questions were as yet unanswered...

Stay patient my friends, for all will come!

20

Islands in the Storm

"All around the world, as the Great Realignment strips away the old consciousness, there will appear 'Islands' - multi-dimensional places - to where spiritual people would be drawn and, as much as possible, protected from the worst of the realigning deluge to come."

I was flying on the out-stretched wings of Pegasus - the mythical horse that carries souls between Earth and heaven. Only this time, it was Pegasus the Turkish charter company, and I was flying in an aircraft! The point is, I'd booked the flight through an online agency, and didn't know I'd be flying with Pegasus until I boarded the craft. Before you awaken, I know such synchronicities wouldn't even register, or if they did, perhaps with only an ironic laugh and a joke. However, when you unfold back into multi-dimensionality, the universe will use every possible method to tune you back into its mother tongue. Like for example, the security firm "Orion", who were controlling ground security for the interconnecting flight into Mesopotamia, my next destination: Orion being a key source of the Opposing Consciousness. These 'metaphoric interplays' don't just happen by chance; in the Divinicus reality, there is no such thing as a coincidence.

I was travelling out to the ancient archaeological site of Göbekli Tepe, in the heart of Mesopotamia, between the biblical rivers Euphrates and Tigris. It's just a stone's throw North from the warring turbulence of Syria. If there was indeed an Ark that carried Noah's family and the animals to safety, some speculate it came to rest on Mount Ararat, just a couple of days journey to the

East. It was the extraordinary carvings on the temple pillars that drew me: mystical creatures, carved with a great sense of empathy, deep respect and love. You had the sense that there was something other-worldly and very sacred, about Göbekli Tepe.

It's a site that sits on top of a mountain ridge *(some speculate seven hills, mirroring in layout, the seven sisters of the Plaiedes).* And as I wound my way up through the arid landscape, the main 'dig' was sitting on top of hill number five; the numeral '5' having been carved into the hillside - presumably, by the archaeologists working the site. Yet again, the probable significance of the Five Gateways was already spiking in my awareness: there was that "aha" sense, that stirs a wry smile, lighting up your heart. So what would this site be about? Clearly the signs were already pointing to some kind of Ascension portal.

What I came to love about Göbekli Tepe, is that it completely defies convention and accepted mainstream 'wisdom'. At 11,000 years old, it must have been built after the 'Great Flood', that swept across the Earth, at the end of the last Ice Age. The traditional historical record, about human population, is that advanced civilisation developed with the Sumerians at around 5000 BC, in the same general area. So when a humble farmer discovered the tip of one of Göbekli Tepe's two hundred intricately carved pillars, protruding out of the ground, the site must have become an unwelcome thorn in the side of all those with vested interests in the traditional view. It can only have been an advanced civilisation that built this, yet several thousand years earlier, when man was still meant to be living in the 'stone age' *(how it reminded me of the chromosome inconvenience, that mainstream science would also rather sweep under the proverbial rug!).*

The fact that this huge, elevated site had been purposefully buried under tonnes of sandy earth, was yet another reason, why Göbekli Tepe has generated such intriguing mystery. Who was trying to hide it, and what were they trying to hide exactly? *Maybe the 'boys' from Orion weren't too keen on this place either!*

As I wandered through the site, a deep sense of reverence and empathic love arose effortlessly within me, as if one of the many carved birds was sweeping me aloft. Yes, those who built this, must have had a deep respect and admiration for animals. But the creature that intrigued me most, was a carving that looked suspiciously like a crocodile, pointing downwards into the earth - *'their representation of the raptor consciousness?' I wondered. Maybe this was a last bastion of Original Humanity, leaving a message about the Intervention that had swept across the Earth like a plague? Maybe it was a portal of Ascension into the heavens - maybe an 'Island in the Storm'?*

Göbekli Tepe is now a popular tourist attraction, but fortunately, at one key point, the small crowd cleared away, leaving the site empty, and as the sun began to smile through the cloudy skies, I settled quickly into a deeply sublime meditation. The speed with which the vibrational resonance opened me up confirmed it: *yes, it was some kind of island in the surrounding storm of consciousness; yes, it was a portal, effortlessly sweeping me into the higher paradigm of the Fifth Density.* And it still retained much of its elevational power today, despite having been purposefully buried for thousands of years. No wonder the Intervention didn't want people finding and working with this site. Just like other 'Islands in the Storm' that you can find around the world, this would have had a deeply realigning impact on those who used it, punching a gaping hole in the matrix.

I was reflecting on this some while later *(Pegasus having flown me back to the UK)* whilst at a similar sacred site on Dartmoor - a rugged, untouched and untainted stretch of moorland in South West England. Although the countryside is very different, the sense of unviolated 'Island in the Storm' was equally palpable. And it too has hosted many an advanced spiritual culture, for very similar reasons to Göbekli Tepe. I could well imagine a universal connection between the Druids of the moors, and the Shamans who must have carved those Mesopotamian pillars. On this particular day, I'd been guided to a stream, to meditate on a boulder in mid-current. It was a staring-eye meditation, and very quickly, I got the sense of being completely at one with the rushing water, as its cleansing energy gushed right through me. It was then that Gaia spoke to me, clearly, once again - *but of course not in words.*

My attention was spiked and drawn to other boulders in the stream. I strongly got the sense, that the stream was representing the great flow of realignment, as it swept unclean energy away. But what was the significance of the boulders?...

All around the world, as the Great Realignment strips away the old consciousness, there will appear 'Islands' - multi-dimensional places - to where spiritual people would be drawn and, as much as possible, protected from the worst of the realigning deluge to come. Those with the emerging Divinicus consciousness, would come together in self-supporting communities, and use the remaining time to help as many as possible shift into the higher paradigm. These Islands in the Storm would be as 'arks' for humanity's Ascension.

Of course the Intervention has always been very ingenious. Thus far, it's developed ever more technologically sophisticated means to overcome the natural harmony of life. Surely this situation would be no different? The powers-that-be would undoubtedly seek all manner of ways in which to avoid the inevitable, to continue their fear-based agenda? Clinging to the surface in geodomes perhaps; transhumanistic cities carefully controlled by geo-engineering; or else burrowing deep into the earth, creating underground caverns. I came to realise all of these were **already** a part of their synthetic reality agenda. Whatever, it didn't seem to matter. Because like the Hopi Elders, I too had the sense that in order to survive what was to come, you'd have to be interconnected, very awake, and realigned with the natural path of the divine. So how would these final elements of resistance be dealt with? *How would the cancer* *be completely purged from the Earth?* For only this would establish a new foundation stone - *a cleansed core* - on which to unfold the New Paradigm, one without the violation of the Intervention.

And then I saw it: a combination of ancient knowings I'd previously had access to; a connection with imagery, feelings and lucid dreams, one of which, was shared in the Gateway 3 experience of Five Gateways. Many had been seeing the sign '11:11' leading up to the all important solstice of 2012 *(in fact, I still often see it, as I'm sure others do too)*. But to me, it was never about a particular time (as had been speculated). It was to do with the alignment of four key centres of consciousness: the galactic core, the soul of our sun (the "Solar Logos"), that of Gaia, and last but not least, the devic souls of ascending sentient life on our planet. Alignment of these key centres, had been the 'trip switch' that initiated the final centering of Gaia's consciousness in the Fifth Density.

*This crucial event marked a unique turning point in her history, which would be like no other transition she had previously undertaken. **In short, she had processed her karma.** The immense significance of this cannot be over-stated. She has released, and moved past, the trauma of her early 'protoplanet' incarnation. She has forgiven herself for the five mass extinctions. As any sense of devic guilt fell away, she was clear to release the karmic ballast of energy she'd been carrying: she no longer needs the controlling matrix, which has been interwoven in her Fourth Density field, by her very own requirement. As this density now begins to peel away, it will render the Intervention without energetic foundation. Any sentient life still attached to that karmic layer, **when it passes on,** will be drawn away from the Earth. As Gaia continues the Ascension and Great Realignment, she will be as accommodating as possible to all her children, but definitely not weak. With help from the other devic souls - including the Solar Logos - she will firmly do, what now has to be done.*

As this landed within me, with tears in my eyes, I saw visions of the old karma being stripped away from her, *like a snake, peeling away a redundant and worn out skin.* And this fourth dimensional energy layer, now devoid of anchoring connection into the heart of Gaia, would be pulled through space-time into the galactic core, to be fragmented into shreds of consciousness - *'elementals'* - before being thrust out the other side, thus providing physical material to take on form in another galaxy. Yes, this is what I had known before. This was the ancient knowledge, that had until now, evaded me: *the universe continually manifests karmic distortion so that realities can form and self-realisation happen; but where those distortions become too convoluted, too 'screwed up', then their density is ultimately drawn into a universal 'washing machine' - a super-dense, galactic black hole, which strips that consciousness apart.*

Yes I'd seen it in Five Gateways, but until this point, I'd not finally put all the pieces together. So this is what it now meant to me:

Gaia's final cleansing will be through a 'fever'. As she ascends, her magnetic energy field will dwindle, exposing the 3D biosphere to intense solar activity, which will change the very nature of the atmosphere. This is what 'the falling of the skies' quote meant to me back in the Hopi Lands of Arizona.

She will heat up, sweat water from her tired brow, sneeze wind and storm across the face of the Earth, break up the very surface, to cleanse away the virulent, cancerous Intervention that had so taken ahold. But she would be compassionate. Islands in the Storm would reveal themselves to all those who had remembered how to see with inter-dimensional eyes.

During this process, as it unfolds, a newly divine consciousness would be born within humanity: souls would be drawn here with greater respect and at-one-ment with all life. They would help as many as possible remember their sacred connection to the Source, to come together and support one another as they prepare for the miraculous shift into the higher paradigm.

This cleansing process in the lower realm will not be pretty, for all those with vested interest in the old fear-based reality. They will still undoubtedly try to shape and control in some 'New World Order'. But it will be short-lived: over time, their number will die off, as either their souls experience 'dissolution' through the galactic core, or else are healed and realigned with the Source. Ultimately, the 3D Earth will 'condense' down, into a core foundationary 'stone' - a 'seed' around which the higher dimensional existence will be shaped.

Yes, I could finally see it. It all made sense. The knowing that I had prior to my incarnation came flooding back to me. Although I knew the changes would be felt as catastrophic by many, it would provide the most compassionate vehicle, by which to bring the balance of the Earth's collective consciousness back into harmony. And all those realigning, would have nothing to fear: even death would result in passing on - to a new life in a realigned incarnation. Over time, increasingly, the plague that has so poisoned the Earth and humanity, will be purged away. This is what the Hopi meant when they said it would be a 'war' on materiality. Because although there is not one vengeful bone in Gaia's body, *this is what it would seem like on the surface, as she sheds the redundant layers, and reconstitutes herself.*

I swallowed these realisations as an intensely bitter-sweet pill. Like many I'm sure, I won't be sad to see the demise of the raptor consciousness on Earth, the dog-eat-dog, predator and prey mentality. But this 'survival of the fittest' has also evolved the most superlative specimens of materiality. Of course that couldn't be wrong, it's how life continually shapes into new form...

And that's exactly the point: in an Ascending Universe, moving to ever higher harmonies, sentient life learns from its lessons of the past, embodying the awareness, but moving on to existences where life-forms support one another. In the next vibrational Fifth Density, they co-create in harmony; they don't exploit life at the suffering expense of another.

So we must now be brave and have the courage to let go of fear. We must work not to control our lives, or manipulate the surface of the Earth, but allow this Great Realignment to confront us with our attachments - our limiting hooks into the old reality. These ties are what create identity and make us small. We must seize every opportunity, to gloriously break apart those bonds - *inside ourselves* - and expand into the divine beings that we are. Thus every challenge we're likely to face, holds the silver lining of an incredible opportunity... *spiritual mastery.* Above all, we must transcend the need for some particular, physical outcome, in the microcosm of our lives. Instead, we must learn to trust again in the benevolence of the universe - that it knows best, what is in the highest interests of not just ourselves, but all life.

And so, over the course of time, this shift will become tumultuous, offering this evolutionary opportunity to every single man, woman and child on the planet. The Earth is to become a crucible of metamorphosis. So called 'geo-engineering' by the powers-that-be will not help, in any way shape or form. Whilst the ultimate conclusion is already now pre-determined, the magnitude of the intermediary shifts set to come, will be unpredictable and uncontrollable. Humanity's ability to live in large collectivised cities, depending on industrial agriculture and globalised resource chains, over the next few decades, will come under ever increasing pressure. To prosper in this shift, humanity must transcend his base physical desires, his addiction to the limiting matrix, and rediscover his divine connection to the heart of Gaia - *now in the Fifth Density.* Money, greed, unnecessary possessions or over-consumption will only hinder. These are merely investments - *anchoring hooks* - into the old reality, which over time, is to be peeled away and fragmented - *composted* - through the galactic cleansing process. No matter how high and mighty, *no one who is still connected to this control-based consciousness, will escape the tumultuous process.* Control, of course, is based on an inherent sense of lack. And what you conceal within, ultimately manifests a mirror: *controllers are controlled by their own limitation.*

Perhaps that's why it's been prophesied *'the meek shall inherit the Earth'?* For me, the word 'humble' would be much more appropriate than 'meek' - and with humility, but not weakness. We must cultivate the will of the warrior to surrender into the shift, and the compassion of the divine feminine to endure it with grace; it will take passionate courage, to stand as an example, to all those still struggling in the collapsing old world. Just as I'm sure many of you reading have also felt, I've seen an evolved humanity graciously abandon the exploitative - *globalised* - ways of society, and come together in self-supporting communities - *Islands in the Storm* - that respect the sanctity of the Earth, including all life here:

For even as the old-world dies, to transcend it, is to become as-one with it, by cherishing the very fibre of it.

So there is nothing to fear, except our attachment - *our fear* - itself. Actually our fear - which contracts people down - **is** the path to expansive liberation, rebirthing you as a universal being. Just as the Shamans did at the sacred site of Göbekli Tepe, and others have at many other multi-dimensional 'Islands' around the world, humanity must come of age by evolving back to his spiritual self.

'How much time did he have?' I wondered. And then the Team spoke to me, just as clearly as they had done so many times before - with signs and synchronicity, that resonated deep within me... *'We're currently living in two worlds, the higher overlapping the lower; but the light of consciousness is now progressively shifting into the New World. The Earth's bio-magnetic energy field will dwindle over time. Solar activity will transform the biosphere, and by a varied mechanism of progressive shifts, leave a purified 'seed' - a foundation for the higher dimensional reality. Although the final alignment will take thousands of years to condense and settle, by 2100, the turn of the century, all sophisticated physical life will cease in the 3D.'*

Thus humanity - those ready to embrace our evolutionary Journey of Ascension - must now come swiftly of age.

21

Humanity Comes of Age

"The Baboon Alpha male was now clearly in sight:
barking loudly; thumping the ground in front of him;
darting through the trees, down the valley side,
on a path that was unfortunately, very convergent with mine!"

Enosh the Zulu emerged out of the early morning mist at the track junction where we'd agreed to meet, at exactly the appointed hour. I'd employed him through Michael Tellinger's Zulu Planet organisation in Mpumalunga. The archaeologist is famous for his exploration of some pretty amazing and as yet, fairly unknown archaeological sites in South Africa. I'd come first to see a site known as 'Adam's Calendar', an ancient stone circle, that seemed to have some poignant cosmic alignments - *notably Orion* - and considered by Michael to be at least 75,000 years old (estimated by weathering of the stones).

According to Enosh, Zulu tribes had used this site to conduct ceremony for thousands of years, and indeed I could sense it still had a powerful energy, as we explored and meditated there together. It was immediately clear to me, that with cosmic energy spiralling into it, there was much more to the site, than just the observation of planetary alignments. It felt more like a stargate, to bring astral travellers in. My attention was drawn to three fallen stones, pointing west, into the vast open plain that Adam's Calendar looks out onto. *And there in the distance, were two pyramid shaped 'mountains' which compelled me very strongly.* So just an hour later, I'm bouncing around on an extremely rough and dusty track, heading out in their direction, the suspension of the neat, little hire car being tested to the limit. At least I could empathise with it: my bones had, by now, been rattled by countless miles of globe trotting!

It was worth it. As the two pyramids came into view, it suddenly became clear, that there was a third, smaller, but clearly visible, and in a very similar alignment to Orion's Belt. Their shape was remarkably pyramid-like. They were not at all natural - standing out like three sore thumbs on the otherwise open landscape. Michael confirmed it for me: yes, they were aligned as Orion's Belt, and what's more, on the same longitude as the Egyptian 'Great' Pyramids. So what were these structures doing in South Africa? What was also profoundly intriguing, were the ruins in the area, of tens of thousands of round stone buildings: *together, amounting to the size of a vast modern-day city, sitting on top of the main gold fields of South Africa.* Unlike their famous Egyptian cousin, just a few thousand miles further to the north, these ancient and mysterious relics were practically unknown to the mainstream - *how strange!*

This intrigue swirled in my mind as I stood in one of the circles: *what effect might they have?* The first thing I noticed was a strong buzzing in my brain, and the feeling of separation between left and right - intellect and intuitive cognition. Although I sensed the site was no longer really active, it still retained some of its original purpose; *I had the strong feeling of a reordering wanting to take place at a DNA level.* It's like the rational was being separated from the intuitive; male from the female. And I felt a strong blocking sensation in my throat chakra too - a kind of 'woolliness'. For me, the throat chakra connects directly into higher mind, so it felt like some degree of reordering - *downgrading* - was taking place. Understandably, I didn't feel to stay in the circles too long!

As I sat with Michael some while later, at his Zulu Planet community, he was sharing ideas that the site was all about Annunaki gold mining. That may have been the case, in part. However, I couldn't help thinking - they were mining not just precious metal, *but precious genes too!* Then it came to me, landing as a knowing: *this was where the original downgrading took place; it's why the mitochondrial DNA of Homo Sapiens points back to this same area some 200,000 years ago.* But what were the stone circles all about? Without doors and windows, it didn't make sense for them to be houses.

I was now deep in an inter-dimensional dialogue, it didn't take long for the following knowing to land: *these were portals into the 'sky'; they were the doorways into a higher, fourth dimensional 'city'; humans were taken 'off-world' - abducted - and then genetically hybridised.* I wondered if this site had something to do with the legendary 'Atlantis?' At first it didn't make sense; many spiritual people have fond recollections of Atlantean times. But then I realised: many of these would be starsouls, come here to experience the incredible beauty and abundance of the physical Earth. During the Atlantean epoch, before the last Ice Age, human civilisation spread throughout the four corners of the globe, fuelled by highly advanced - *alien* - technology. Not everyone would have immediately appreciated - *or witnessed* - the brutal hybridisation that preceded it. It wasn't until it spun out of control *(just as in today's society)*, that a catastrophic realignment became necessary, in the form of the Great Flood. Which is why researchers are now finding evidence of the ancient Atlantean civilisation, all around the world, yet submerged below the water.

It felt to me, like this African site, had been the central pillar of the Altantean civilisation. This was my background chain of thought, as I sat with Michael, but wasn't yet ready to share. Because suddenly, a loud crackling sound distracted our attention - *burning red fire burst into the air in the field opposite us!* Within minutes, waves of five metre high flames swept across the fields, destroying all in their path. These things don't happen by chance: synchronicity speaks volumes. Just as 'God' had apparently spoken to Moses, these *'burning bushes'* were revealing a clear message, about how the universe responds to such Intervention: *it sweeps it from the Earth, just as the Great Flood had swept away Atlantis.*

The cleansing fire delivered not only an important message, but a welcome sense of realignment; just as fields are frequently burned to inspire new growth *(yet another poignant metaphor of what I believed was now to come)*. Fortunately, Michael's community had been protected from the fire, by a very conveniently located stream. My heart was warmed, that his farm had been spared: *surely an 'Island in the Storm', which Gaia had already spoken of.*

It was further south in Africa that drew me next. There was a clear, heart-felt pull, as if somehow taking me home. As I drove into the area of the Sterkfontein Caves - *for a reason not immediately clear* - rivers of tears sprang from weary eyes, and washed cleansingly down rosy-red cheeks. Here I am, driving down your typical, busy motorway, the noises and pollution, the insensitivity and ignorance; yet with such an upwelling of scared warrior emotion, it felt as if with one primal outcry, I could ripple all that uncaring carnage away.

The caves are undoubtedly majestic, holding a vibrational frequency that deeply resonates in the bosom of Gaia. You get the sense that subtly vibrating sound energy, is gently restoring battered and botched DNA; like resting in a warm volcanic spring, the water gently rippling through weary limbs. I could feel this was where the Original Human story had began. To me, you can see it quite clearly in the fossil record of the museum there. I listened intently, as the tour guide explained: *"this was an area like no other on the planet; it's where you find a huge array of early and varying kinds of Hominid fossils, dating from around four million years ago to around 1 million years ago".* As he spoke, my eyes scanned the throng of modern-day humanity, now listening with mild interest to the story of their roots. It struck me how varied the people all were. With different skin shades, builds and facial features, it was synchronistically astounding: *apart from each having two eyes, ears, arms and legs, not one person looked remotely like any other!*

With the tour guide's continuing dialogue, knowing and memory sparked within my cells: *yes, it was done here -* **the Benevolent** *seeding of Original Humanity; conducted gently, over millions of years, through countless careful iterations, until the right form was perfected; it was done with the help of sound vibration, progressively altering the DNA of the Hominid creatures.* But something didn't sit right within me: there was the faint itch of discomfort. What was that itch?

It's later that evening now, and I'm camped out on top of a mountain, blanketed with sparkling evening stars. The Plaiedes constellation is clearly visible, strong in my awareness. It causes me to reflect on a trip 'down under', in Australia, earlier that year: I'd met many starsouls from the Plaiedes, who for some particular reason, had tended to congregate on Australia's eastern coast. I'd listened closely, with great interest, to a number of stories of space ships landing there, bringing the early human forebears - a story that is intimately enshrined within the Aboriginal culture. What was the connection between Australia and South Africa, the place from where I was now reminiscing? And what about the other star-people on the planet, like the Native Americans, some of whom also speak of descending from the stars? It wasn't easy putting the pieces of the jigsaw back together. The past is long since gone, and although essences remain in the Akashic Record, I'm reminded that the past is still the past, and since all parts of the universe are flowing together, then the energies of particular circumstances no longer exist. Like the fossil remnants in the Sterkfontein caves, only shadows are carried forwards. It's their influences that are important to us now: *how are we being influenced by our history, right now, in this moment?*

As I lay underneath the stars, a quantum shift of energy seemed to project my consciousness instantly back in time. Suddenly it came to me, like a gigantic wave, just why the original seeding had taken place at all. I could recall the original 'thinking'. The Intervention on Earth had already been experienced for many millions of years, the DNA carried here on the meteor 'space-ship', initiated by the ingenious 'intentional panspermia' by the mother species in a far away constellation. I watched the tragic exploitation of the Earth, during the reign of the Dinosaurs, and I saw them bite the dust as another heavenly asteroid struck the Earth. I could feel it was known, that the parasitic 'raptor consciousness', which had spawned their consumptiveness, still remained, and would undoubtedly rise again. *"What could be done?"* I wondered. The solution landed almost immediately.

What was needed was an intelligent creature, a courageous one, that thrived in the dense Earth environment. One that was ready to embody individual soul, so as to channel - ***to ground*** - higher divinity onto the surface of the Earth; thereby to break up the collective consciousness of the Intervention. And what was also needed, was an advanced civilisation to lend a part of their DNA - a species who might also incarnate their starsouls here; to have their own evolving experience and usher in the new humanity. Crucially, they would need to carry a vibration, to *'level the playing field'*, and help unwind the Intervention; a species like the Plaiedians for example, who were already on Earth, occupying a higher vibrational paradigm, *once known as Lemuria*. The Group of Nine - *the Team* - confirmed it for me:

> *Yes, it was known that the Intervention would try to consume and take over this creature. It had happened all too frequently in other constellations. And later, the Group could feel the yearning in the collective Hominid form, for more individualised expression. Their form could be adapted, to suit their evolving needs, and ideally, to also stem the rising tide of the Intervention. Humanity would become the very battle ground, to take on this Opposing Consciousness and try to turn it around, to realign it. It's a battle that would take place in every mind, every cell, every strand of DNA.*

So this great danger to the Earth was ***already*** recognised by Benevolence, even ***before*** humanity was seeded here. Such uncompassionate exploitation had happened many times before, elsewhere in the universe. What was needed was a new 'custodian' of the Earth's surface; one that would ultimately be able to realign the Intervention, not by fighting, *but by the physical embodiment of higher consciousness.* The new species would become a mirror to those opposing energies. Its primary vibration would be one of love and alignment with the divine. No, Benevolence is not naive. As the Team confirmed for me...

> *Yes, it was accepted that Intervention by this Opposing Consciousness would almost certainly happen. But it had also been realised, that unless you bring them back into the light in some way, then you'll simply have to re-engage the problem, at some other time, somewhere else. Why not grasp the prickly thorn now? The best way would be engagement with these entities; present them with a mirror of reconciliation and reconnection to the Source; to convince them that further evolutionary alignment is the only way to bring lasting contentment and fulfilment of what you really desire, at a soul level. Control simply leads to karma, that will surely catch up with you, in some unpleasant guise, further on down the universal track.*
>
> ***If you want to dissolve selfish exploitation in the universe, you must first allow it to succeed, to over-extend itself by it's own 'success', until it becomes brittle and weak. We've discovered through the eons, that's by far the most elegant way of encouraging realignment with the universal fold.***

So it was now clear in my knowing, it **had** been the purpose of Benevolence to populate the planet with a being, who could ultimately provide the vehicle where the Intervention could be engaged, shown a mirror of surrendering truth, and then turned around - realigned with the universal flow.

Actually, it unfolded for me over time, that the mission encapsulated a number of interrelated purposes:

*To help starsouls from across the cosmos to embody, and
thereby re-engage with the process of reincarnation in order
to process karma. Even Opposing Consciousness souls would
be included, as and when they surrendered to the Source.
Meanwhile, the evolving Hominids on Earth were yearning
for greater evolutionary expression. And so a group from
the Plaiedes was chosen to lead the new seeding. Despite
great challenge, over hundreds of thousands of years, the
seeding was successful. Various Hominid adaptations were
facilitated, with DNA frequencies interwoven to create
variant, but related species, that would allow the various
starsouls to incarnate. And thus, to cut a long and complex
story short, Original Hominids became Original Humans,
with both Earth souls and a wide variety of starsouls
embodied.*

As I currently understand it, the overriding theme, was to unite
spiritual aspiration, with the need to unravel and harmonise the
convolutions of the past. And it wasn't that Benevolence was
'playing God', it was more a facilitation - *an easing* - of shifts that
were already naturally beginning to happen. As this knowing
landed for me, there was a poetic sense to it: *variant souls all
embodied in the same vehicle...*What better way to humble? What
better way to empathise? What better way to rekindle the natural
brother and sisterhood principle of the universe: *bring variant,
sometimes opposing factions together, in the same vehicle, looking
very similar, with very similar problems.* To me, there could be
no better way to eventually heal and unify. Because to attain any
kind of harmony in life, they would simply have to overcome their
differences and unite by their commonality.

Starsouls such as the Plaiedians and Sirians embodied perfectly
well; even others, such as the realigning Annunaki and Orion souls,
could also successfully reincarnate into the new form. But it was
recognised that they would all bring with them their various karma

to work through - it was never going to be an easy journey for this new, universal child. So I could also feel the sense of discomfort with the 'plan', one that would be passed on to a suitable group of starsouls to help carry out; ones that also had experience of the Intervention, who would continually remind the Original Humans of their divine connection. The Plaiedians fitted the bill perfectly.

It wasn't an intentional plan as such. The Group does not work that way. Rather it helps bring the threads of an already emerging story together; then to catalyse it more rapidly to it's rightful conclusion. Ideally, removing as much unnecessary pain and suffering as possible.

However, as the Intervention took a furious hold on these Original Humans and their Plaiedian mentors, I had the feeling that for a long time, the Team was burdened deeply by the sense that they had failed. It would be a profoundly educational process for them too: *When is it right and timely to intervene in the natural evolutionary process of the universe? Was it right to intervene at all?*

This complex conundrum was reverberating in my mind the very next morning, after I'd awoken early from a restless sleep and was making my way along a beautiful, winding riverbank. Steep and wooded valley sides blocked out any sense of civilisation. It was as if the meandering riverbank, was slipping me nonchalantly back in time...

Suddenly, there's a loud 'barking' noise up above me on the valley side. A shadow darts amongst the trees. Then two, three, four, and increasingly more of them. What on Earth were they? Their energy was moving ever closer. I could feel them long before I could see them: primal; muscle pumping; agitated. The Baboon Alpha male was now clearly in sight: barking loudly; thumping the ground in front of him; darting through the trees, down the valley side, on a path that was unfortunately, very convergent with mine!

I bend down to grasp a rock, with which to defend myself,
should I need to; and as I stand up, suddenly he's there in
front of me, barely twenty metres away. Face to face, past and
future. What was it that I could make out in those creature's
eyes? What was the reflection I was now feeling? As I felt the
rock in my hand, anger and resentment hung in the air's tense
stillness between us; at least that's how my own sense of guilt
and responsibility interpreted it. For all the pain, challenge
and hardship, there was the undeniable feeling that we - I -
had badly screwed up. And here in front of me, was the result
of that: a creature marginalised; clinging to life as its habitat
is mercilessly 'civilised' in front of its eyes. How civil does a
motorway, an airport or a city look to a Baboon, I wonder?
How civil is it when you can no longer find food nor shelter for
your family? And perhaps the beginnings of the question in the
Baboon's mind: "Why would Great Spirit allow such a thing?"

As I looked deep into his eyes, it was as if I could see right back
to the beginnings of the universe, to the 'Original Mistakes';
awareness getting lost in the illusion, controlling reality and then
revelling in physicality. In the highest realms of consciousness, it
was just a glitch in the flow, no one's fault, it was inevitable - it
just happened. Nevertheless, the result of this confusion, of this
lack of self-realisation, of this entanglement, must then manifest
outwards and cascade downwards; taking on all manner of form
and circumstance to confront and unravel the distortion. That's
how the universe naturally works. Thus billions of years of history
flashed through my consciousness: Earth, trying to embody in
those early protoplanet hours; Sirius B exploding in shafts of white
light during her White Dwarf Ascension, the beings of nearby
planets shattered and torn apart; I saw the early incarnations on
Earth, which gave me great joy, and the Intervention, which did
not; then I watched in amazement, as galactic alignment spurred
on Gaia's more gentle Ascension; and now, the powerful cleansing
to heal the cancer that has so poisoned her. In that moment,
time had temporarily frozen, as billions of years of creation -

and unravelling distortion - rippled its way from the far reaches of the universe, gathering energy, taking on all manner of form; *eventually resulting in a great ape, now standing intently before a once great human.*

It's only ego that apportions blame. As I recall this superlative experience, my mind reflects back to a film, "Good Will Hunting". It's about a young and angry man, growing up in rough times, with the spark of brilliance that the world so desperately tries to stamp out. What does a young mind do in such a hostile environment, abandoned by a very absent God? In the beginning, there's much outwardly projected aggression, until eventually, the finger of blame starts to point inwards - to the causality: *only I can be the source of all this anguish; it can be only me.* Responsibility for our choices is of course a good thing, but when that becomes twisted with guilt and self-blame, then all manner of distorted behaviour takes form. As his counsellor looks deeply into the eyes of young Will, and tells him, *"It's not your fault"*, first he tries to turn away; his pain and resentment is all he can cling to, when the loving embrace of God had become so distant. Yet here was that compassion once more, in the softly spoken, caring voice, *"It's not your fault"*. "Yes I know," is Will's reply, but as yet, it's only at the coping level of ego; excuses and avoidances - blame projected outwards onto someone else, just as so many people do. *"It's not your fault,"* with deeply loving eyes. And now, the statement penetrates deep into the emotional body. Suddenly, waves of pent-up resistance and isolation spring from weary eyes. A soul that had journeyed through the eons, lost in a spiral of isolation from God, due to its own self-blame, starts to come home. *And likewise I say to you reading, that for all the things you may feel you've done in your life: for all the aggressiveness and victimisation; the wrongdoings, mistakes, failures and selfishness...* **"It is not your fault!"**

This is the process that unwound itself in me, as I stood before this great ape. How ever I had been involved in this rediscovery process; how ever the Group of Nine had seeded Original Humanity; how ever the universe had entwined the Original Mistakes, manifested now as the Intervention - **none of us were to blame!** We were all merely actors on a great stage. In that moment, it didn't matter what happened next; I didn't need to defend myself; I could accept the destiny of the universe for me. And so I let the rock slip from my hand. And as I did so, *could I see a softening in those sorrowful and angry eyes? Indeed, I thought I did.*

The baboon cautiously backed off, leaving me to continue my winding path along the river, its meandering flow helping integrate the gentle flooding of past knowing and realisation. Back at the beginning of this re-acquaintance story, I spoke of the undeniable coding within the chromosomes of man: the 48 of the great apes that had, in some inexplicable way, become 46 in humanity. And how those other nine chromosomes had somehow, mysteriously, been inverted. 'Why nine?' I wondered. *"Because we're accepting responsibility"* was the answer that softly cascaded into my mind:

> *It's a hidden code, buried for those who will eventually find the key. In us - the Group of Nine - taking responsibility for the Original Mistakes, means that no one has to load themselves with any kind of blame. For whatever happens, it is not your fault. And neither is it the fault of the Opposing Consciousness. But it is your responsibility to work to unravel those distortions that affect you. Your awakened choices become your sense of purpose. Although we accept responsibility, we do not accept blame either. There is no such thing as a 'mistake': only when you fail to learn from the distortions that the universe itself has created.*

So all along, it was the Group of Nine's idea: the *realisation* to originate humanity with subtle DNA changes, caused by resonating sound, that were then secured in place with nine chromosome inversions. They had done so with the help of Plaiedian starsouls, who were skilled in such seeding. And this new configuration, was then seeded at various locations around the Earth to begin populating it. Which is why some will speak of the 'multi-regional' evolution of Original Man. But then something else happened: a new Homo Sapiens, that had been downgraded in "Atlantis" - *with its centre in Southern Africa* - hundreds of thousands of years later; one that would travel out of Africa, and compelled by their Opposing Consciousnesss concubines, take over the Earth. In the process, *they all but stamped out the Original Human in us.*

All the while, it was known that the Intervention of this Opposing Consciousness would likely rise and take ahold of the new emergent species. It was they who quite brutally downgraded humanity, spliced in limitation, and with a form of laser light, merged the second and third chromosomes, so that their manipulations would be secured in place. Thus, disconnected from God, they'd inculcate a new 'paternalism', living their lives through the energy fields of the newly enslaved Homo Sapiens. As incredible as it may now seem, it was known that this would likely happen.

And at the right time, when the vibration of the Earth had risen once again, an infusion of higher light would reconnect the consciousness of mankind to its original Source. So, in every thought and emotion, in every cell, as you ground and embody this higher consciousness, it must come with a sense of forgiveness and compassion: that no one is at fault for what has taken place; no one is to blame. Even the entities that have so controlled and downgraded you, were merely playing out the Original Mistakes, as awareness plunged itself into the forming universe. Yes, you can each be a part of this unravelling flow: first by liberating yourself from isolation, from any sense of guilt or blame. And as you hold that new sense of Divinicus freedom within your awareness, you're doing the very same thing to any entity that might have invaded, or still be occupying, your field. You're giving them permission to realign and come home too.

To help all on their way - *speedily, to the new dawning* - each must now learn to master the ancient 'Alchemy of Transcendence'.

22

Alchemy of Transcendence

"You have to plunge into the deep-end of life's swirling torrent; unwind, master, and infuse through it. Upon which, you liberate the unbridled fullness of the One that you are - it simply bursts through you, and shines like the sun, into the outer world."

It was now the middle of 2013, and we were back up in the mountains of Snowdonia in North Wales - the celtic retreat centre called "Cae Mabon". The Sweat Lodge fire had been burning away for several hours; the jembe and didgeridoo were serenading us, building the sense of primal connection to ancient Gaia. The deva of the fire danced upon naked flesh, warming it, and at times burning the hairs on it; lest we become complacent, thinking this is going to be just another walk in the park - just another spiritual ceremony. We entered the lodge on hands and knees, a humbling and intimate connection with the earth, which now merged with the smoke of the fire on sweating skin. Suddenly it's pitch black. Crammed shoulder to shoulder with your nervous compatriots, you can see absolutely nothing. The invitation is to feel as deeply as you can, there's no other choice, nowhere else to go, nowhere to hide. You're now in the bosom of the Earth, and as the glowing red rocks are hoisted into the fire pit at the heart of the lodge, the inner volume and intensity are suddenly magnified ten-fold. *You're right in the crucible of alchemical change, and there's no avoiding it.*

Each has to deal with their own inner demons: fear, lack of trust, identification with the physical; the smoke that stings your watery eyes, and the heat that burns your lungs. Thoughts kick off: *'maybe I won't make it through; I'm not good enough to be here; I'll make a fool of myself in front of everyone else.'* It's all the ingrained stuff, the baggage that people carry around in their psyche, hardly realising it. Society is so disempowering: it has many soft shoulders to placate this self-victimisation upon. In the Sweat Lodge, you just can't avoid the close proximity of your own weakness. So you have to work with it; which means to go into the very heart of it. You have to accept it completely and become as one with the pain, otherwise it becomes overwhelming.

And it's not about fighting either. It's about surrender. I've watched many a warrior male, collapsed in a sobbing heap on the floor, as the divine feminine consoles him. You see this is the point: *pain only becomes suffering when you try to avoid or fight it; in other words, when you become an identity trying to suppress it.* In that instant, you become less than the divine being that you are, and instead, a much smaller identity.

There are basically two types of consciousness that make up your being - your essential experience of the One: there's the separation consciousness that forms the bodymind; and then unity consciousness that forms the soul. As the soul, you are a unique expression of the One, which when liberated and flowing freely, has no limitation. So that's the name of the game - *of all games:* to find, attune and liberate the soul's glorious expression. There is literally nothing else, that is real, going on; everything else is distorted illusion. Yes, there's believing yourself - *intellectually* - to be the One; but this can only be truly known, *through* the experience of relativity - *your soul relative to something else.*

The soul carries a frequency that is uniquely you. Upon incarnation, by the Law of Attraction, you manifest a body and the circumstances of your life. These become the mirrors that reflect - *as an inner feeling* - both the aligned authenticity of your soul, and where you become distorted. Here's the point: *if you become identified with the physicality in some way (which includes distancing through denial), then you make that physicality a real experience for you - the heat of the moment now defines you.* In effect, you're accepting your limitation. Since consciousness defines your experience, you're now attuning to, and being defined by, the separation consciousness; the light of the soul is fragmented and dimmed by it. Within your being, you literally become that limitation...

And this is exactly what happened to the Ancient Lemurians
- those that activated the seed of the Original Human.

It was intensely hot, like a crucible of burning transformation. The trials and the tribulations of everyday life had long since dissolved, as if into some distant galaxy; you had no choice but to confront what was happening to you. I needed to ease the pain somewhat, it was simply too strong. So I carefully scrunched myself up, lying down on the ground, closer to the cooling earth of Gaia. She was a gentle, consoling mother, and I was her vulnerable baby, now in the feotal position. Yes, it did feel very much like a birthing process, but not just this incarnation - because after some minutes, I was projected back in time. Initially it was confusing, hazy, but then I remembered: *it felt like the intensely challenging situation of being born as one of the Original Humans.*

Now, I could mostly remember; not with absolute clarity, they were more feelings and knowings. They were accompanied by visual flashbacks, but also a deep inner knowing, that what I was now recalling had a strong degree of truth: it was our role to come in, *with our spirit light bodies,* to pave the way by resonating a particular frequency of vibration. I was to act as an emissary between the Team I know, the deva of the hominid species we were embodying into, and the Lemurian starsouls who would take up the initial seeding challenge...

Together, by a collective yearning for evolutionary growth,
we would birth the new human form by resonating our soul
frequency within the hominid being. Thus human souls,
who were beginning to separate as individuals from the

devic consciousness, could begin to incarnate into the new, individualised form. For the Original Humans, it would be ecstatic - individual consciousness embodied in a superlative vehicle. But for us, it was a double-sided coin: the joy of the physicality yes, but with the growing sense of disconnection, which the density also causes.

In the lodge, at times, I could hear a resonant sound that so reminded me of a previous existence - *the Lemurian Seventh Dimensional Realm I'd originally incarnated on Earth to.* The resonance was comforting, and seeming to emanate from outside the lodge - outside the womb. It was aligning my soul, by retaining the spirit-light-body vibration, as it embodied into the denseness of physical form. I could recall the ancient Lemurians and their attraction to lowering their vibration into physicality; to partake of the physical pleasures of the world, to bite of the 'apple' and taste its juices on a human tongue. *And yes, we knew the slippery snake of the Intervention would be waiting, to tempt and engross the Lemurians in the physical. That's what it does; that's its purpose, as the manifestation of the Original Mistake.* I could feel now the acute intimacy of the 'doubled-sided coin'. Yes, incarnation in this human form would be awesomely physical, *awesomely real.* Yet I also found it acutely limiting, a bit like being crammed into a straightjacket, one with frequencies that just weren't me. And it was disconnecting: I felt isolated and abandoned. It was not just the past I was feeling, but the present too.

This is what the Lemurians had felt way back when. There was the pleasure of physical incarnation, yes, a bounteous world of beauty. But it was strongly tinged with the sense of creative disempowerment. In contrast, I could recall the higher vibrational existence, in the Seventh Density, with soul brothers and sisters drawn from across the cosmos; a brotherhood of light, come together to experience Earth's splendid treasures, and to assist in the original seeding of humanity. We lived purely on light, assimilating energy from the surrounding field. We could blend with creatures, know what they were feeling, telepathically communicate into their souls. We could flow with the stream, swim with the dolphin, and soar with the eagle. We knew intimately, how to ride the ceaseless flow of divine creation, like a cascading waterfall through our lives. Every moment was a bounteous learning, discovery and expression of our innate selves. No one suffered a sense of lack or disconnection. We were living in an orchestra of streaming synchronicity, like a choir of angels singing non stop, just for us. Right now, losing all of that, felt like a heavy price to pay. But I knew it was worth it, to be of divine service, to assist in the seeding of man.

In the Sweat Lodge, I could feel the pressure building inside me, as if it wanted to explode up through my head. I wanted to sit up, but I knew the pain would intensify. Then I got it - *the real point*. I needed to break through this resistance I was feeling. For it was only me, at the soul level, allowing the sense of victimised contraction. So in the final 'round' *(there were four rounds of 'prayer' each lasting about 45 minutes)*, I sat up, and let the heat throb inside my aching head. I could feel all of the conflict of the past going on inside this tightened mind. I could feel the encased genetic karma throughout my body - the various iterations of form, that progressively evolve a great ape into a great human. I can imagine it felt like the internal consciousness of the nymph, breaking down, and reconfiguring, before emerging as the resplendent dragonfly. So I had to penetrate the pain and soften into it. I knew it was time to confront the feeling head on - *not fighting though, but surrendering into*. I had to feel through every nuance of experience: to permeate gently, softly, with patience and persistence - *the divine feminine*. Your mind is screaming *'Stop! Why are you doing this to yourself?'* But still the impetus is to push on, to push through, by feeling through: not with hardness, but softness. By becoming as one with all, the pain no longer defines you: *you've transcended into your spiritual self; you've infused and activated your spirit-light-body - your merkabah - which you're now living within.*

Suddenly there's a breakthrough: I could feel the tightness in my head break, like an overburdened elastic rope. The dam bursts, the light rushes in and the pain instantly vaporises. My light-body is fully infusing, like a wave, washing away all distortion in its path. As I crawled out of the lodge, carefully, cautiously, on wobbly limbs, and sat on a rock next to the rushing nearby stream, it felt like my whole physical body had become porous. The energy of the water was cascading through me; the light through the trees, permeating every cell. My body didn't feel solid any more. It was morphing and shimmering in response to my spirit-light-body, which was now penetrating through it. *I felt just like one of the Ancient Lemurians once more, dancing with joy in home-coming heavens.*

I bathed in that light for some considerable time; drinking it in for all it was worth, before the density of Sapiens slipped surreptitiously back into my consciousness. But this time, it was different. I could still feel the merkabah - *I could still act through it in this plane.* Yes, I enjoy this physical embodiment, but my soul yearns for the higher vibrations... *just as I believe the soul of humanity is now yearning for the higher vibration of interconnection, which is his next chapter. And the activation of his merkabah, is the path to that Ascension.*

I realised my personal experience, mirrored the purge of the old consciousness, that each must now undertake. The Intervention has, *to some varying degree,* temporarily tainted the soul. Each must now reclaim and heal that original soul frequency, by reattuning with the Source - *through transcendence of the physical.* Together, we must support one another, as we penetrate the Intervention that lingers in our cells, and defines the limiting reality. As we expand softly into it, with commitment and surrender, then we eject the contracting, fear-based mentality from within ourselves, and from the Earth. So this is not just an individual service, *but a greater one for the planet also.* Just like a dragonfly, you peel off the old skin and rise 'out of the water', taking flight as the sun strengthens wings of light. This is true alchemy: how to heal the human spirit and prepare it for the next chapter as the divine being. It is the deepest mysticism, the real secret of divine magic: *penetrate every cell of your being, until the infusion of your higher light activates, then burns away, anything that doesn't belong there.*

Gaia has breathed new life into a new world, with distinct reflections of this previous Lemurian Paradigm. She's patiently waiting for souls to take flight and join her there. It's what inspired Chris' Ascension: progressing from an omnivore, to vegan, to fruitarian; and at times, breatharian - *living purely on the breath -* before he moved on. I'm sure many of you have felt something like this too - *the yearning for inner purification* - as you've woken up, and realised the life you created when you were asleep, just doesn't work anymore. Yet at this stage, the old convoluted vibration is still a part of you, and you have to work through it, because aspects of your soul have identified with the old life in some way. It's these distortions that created the downgraded Homo Sapiens. It's these out-dated beliefs, of needing to shape and control, that people must now process out. But you can't do it simply by distancing yourself from it. That's like trying to disown a part of your soul, because the unrealised part of it formed the trap in the first place. You've got to get right into the heat of the distortion, and unravel the density, so as to reclaim, heal and integrate the lost nuggets of soul gold buried there. And this is exactly what I mean by 'Transcendence'.

My experience with this powerful approach of Transcendence, inspired me to develop what I call a 'spiritual compass' for evolving people. Since it came from 'Team Openhand', I call it "Openhandway". We're currently living in two worlds not one - the new infuses the old. But the old reality is steadily, over time, peeling off like a worn out skin, just as the redundant body of Sapiens soon will. So within ourselves, we must navigate the path between the worlds, into the higher paradigm, *by steadily resurrecting our spirit-light-body.* Openhandway is a profound means of dissecting the often conflicting impulses, that go on within the bodymind, as we work to align with the flow of rightness, and perform the necessary alchemy of light. It means that you can unravel distorted density, that still identifies you with the separation consciousness, forming the ego; then instead, embody soul through those circumstances, *feeling its translucent light encasement.* In this way, the light of the soul, and the resonant merkabah vibration, actually changes the very nature of your being. You eject the Intervention from you, and unleash your divinity through it. Thus, like the original alchemists, *we're transforming base metal into pure gold.*

This spiritual compass works something like this:

Open mind: first become the Observer of your physical self. Watch all thought, feeling and emotion. Especially take note of those situations where you get attached and in need of some kind of outcome from the external drama. Such attachments are experienced as: tightening and contracting down, where you're 'owned' by the event. Even if you get caught up in these moments, keep applying the will to observe yourself in them. Let's be clear, the Divinicus in you can accept anything, providing it comes from the divine and is designed to evolve you. It doesn't need any particular outcome, because it is already filled with the sense of completeness. This is what the filters of the ego mask. If you keep observing, there will come a point when you start to know yourself beyond the bodymind, as the absolute 'Seer' of all things.

Open heart: as we keep being the Observer, we begin to loosen the grip of the ego. This means the soul can flow into the bodymind, especially through those situations where we would usually tighten down. Instead, you feel the sense of heart opening, infusing a greater connection to unity consciousness, flowing through all circumstances. We can turn up the volume of this glorious feeling, by bringing attention specifically into the five senses: feeling, hearing, tasting, smelling, seeing - with a depth of commitment and presence that we've not experienced before. The soul is now infusing further, and we start to feel the natural impulsive direction of the universe, as the landing of higher knowing and a pull through the heart: "this is the way to go now." Your spirit-light-body is beginning to activate.

Receiving hand: *the key is to understand where this heart-felt pull is taking you. It wants to expand you; it wants to reacquaint you with the divine. But in order to do so, you have to confront the contractions and identifications that squeeze the light of divinity from your being. So, as we receive the energy of the universe flowing into the bodymind, the pull will manifest all those circumstances in the outer drama, where we would close down and get stuck: where we get fearful, tight and worried. It is in these moments, that we have to feel the pain of the contraction; and not shrink back. Instead honour it, by fully expressing it, going deeply into the feeling of it. If we keep penetrating the pain, with deep intimacy and consciously expanding through it, then the bubble of contraction will burst. You'll then feel yourself dropping into the Void of infinite potential - the Pure Presence of the Seer - that which you are.*

Giving hand: *as the bubble of identification bursts, and you can accept the perfection of the moment, you'll expand into this inner Void of Presence. Now, for the arising soul, what follows is an expression of 'rightness': it could be the powerful sense of warrior energy; or the divine feminine energy of acceptance. It could be: creative, humorous, passionate, committed, understanding, diplomatic. And as the soul arises, it will do so as a sense of beingness, which is its very purpose. That is, to fully express the magnificence of the One, in every moment, unbridled, unhindered; not needing an outcome. How can any particular external outcome, ever surpass the infusing sense of who you really are? So, give full expression to this authentic sense of you, in whatever way you feel given to, in the moment. Do so without limitation; hold nothing of you back. You're now infusing and unleashing the divine being you are - you're literally infusing your spirit-light-body into you. And now the whole of reality will begin to shape around you; it has no other choice - reality cannot deny the divinity you've become. Celebrate the joy of synchronicity - the divine orchestra - which you then witness, as a constant flowing stream, through your enlightened life.*

This process of Transcendence - this *Openhandway* - is not necessarily as simple as it looks, and it is by no means easy. Being the Observer, for example, in 'Open mind', tends to come and go in the beginning, as you frequently get lost. It doesn't matter, keep reminding yourself to watch. In 'Open heart', patience and persistence are required, taking time out of a conditioned lifestyle to slow down and connect, through softness, into the intimacy of the moment. With 'Receiving hand', often when people feel the pain in some way, be it emotional, mental or physical, the typical reaction is to immediately drop it, placate it, try to take it away; or in the case of karmic pain, to try and blame it on someone else. Keep recognising, accepting and owning the disharmony in your co-creations out in the world. You draw to you, every single situation - *no matter how unpleasant* - for a higher purpose. Embrace the pain and work with it, so that it starts to become pliant and malleable inside. And with 'Giving hand', always make space for your highest truth to express, no matter how the outside world might react to it. Let the truth of who you are, shine through - no matter what.

> *The crucial point, is that by the Law of Attraction, the path is designed to draw to you situations and circumstances, to expose within, the discomfort of attachment: the perceived need for some kind of outcome in the physical world; or else, the non-acceptance of what you've now manifested. It is so you can now feel your contraction, which you can only confront and dissolve in the moment you experience it. You do this by expanding into the tightness that has now been activated and brought into the light. These points of identification, define the spiritual path into the higher vibrational paradigm - into the light-being, Divinicus.*

I've described **Openhandway** in four separate steps. And in the beginning, in order to master it, you'll probably need to approach it in that way: focussing on being the Observer, for example, until you start to feel the heart opening. Writing a daily journal helps to spot the distortions tightening you down, as you receive the realigning energy of the universe. And you'll have to look intently, over a period of time, for those precious gifts of the soul; which, like the spring buds of a previously dormant flower, work to burst through into the rising sun. As you become more adept and skilled at working in this way, the separate stages begin to blend together. Increasingly, you become more able to *catch yourself in the moment*: as soon as any tightness arises, you immediately recognise it, turn to face it, and drop straight into the deep end of it, thus quickly expanding into it, so that it cannot now define your reality. Suddenly, there's a seamless recognition of the emergent soul, which you then give full expression to.

> *And this aligned expression of the soul, is just like focussing a lens: it drops you right into the Source of who you really are: the Void of Presence - the One - the Seer of all things.*

The separate stages then merge into one: you're **always** in a space of surrendered openness, you're **constantly** walking through life processing, expanding, evolving and **unleashing** the divinity within you. You're now walking the inner journey, one which carries you positively, courageously and successfully through the outer world. By activation of your spirit-light-body, you're now streaming as a synchronistic flow through life, as one with the divine, manifesting magic, because of the very embodiment of who you truly are. *What on Earth could be better?*

And to me, it is the most reliable way - *perhaps the only way* - to survive the changes coming, as the old world reality steadily breaks down and peels off. Such Enlightenment becomes a way of life, because you've now realised perhaps the most important, fundamental truth of the universe:

> *other than the unleashing and full expression of your soul, there is absolutely nothing else that is real going on!*

Detachment from life is not an enlightened life. Denying or distancing yourself from any experience simply creates limiting identity around that experience - it makes you less than, smaller than, who you really are. No, to truly know yourself as the eternal One, that is boundless in *any* experience, you have to plunge into the deep-end of life's swirling torrent, denying nor rejecting anything that your consciousness has created in your landscape. Embrace it. Become as one with it. Then unwind, master, and infuse your soul through it. Upon which, you liberate the unbridled fullness of the One that you are - it simply bursts through you, and shines like the sun, through the turbulent dawning of the New World.

How ever challenging it may at first seem to fully grasp this spiritual compass, I can say that each person reading is seeded to master the approach, if you feel so drawn to it. How can I say that with confidence? Well, firstly, because I observe this is the authentic, aligned response to identification with the external universe; I'm merely giving word to what I believe naturally happens as the soul yearns for Enlightenment. It is the inherent motivation to master life - what Pure Presence does, when bottled up inside some kind of illusion. So really, this spiritual compass is simply giving voice to a natural process of evolution that *already* exists in the universe. By 'calling' it in this way, I trust to bring more attention to it, and thereby make the process of inner alchemy more straightforward and easy to integrate. I've now witnessed hundreds of people, in pockets all around the world, successfully applying it. But certainly don't take my word for it - test it, try it for yourself, and see what an incredible transformation it can be.

Speaking from personal experience, I observe it as a powerful pathway to Divinicus. This 'Alchemy of Transcendence', can lead to a totally miraculous life, which will undoubtedly prove essential, in these monumental shifts now taking place. For even as the old world shatters and collapses around us, *it can be as though walking through a continuous miracle.* A path of light opens before you, where you're constantly feeling the uplifting hand of the divine. The old reality is a deliberate delusion of limitation - *a soft shoulder to disempower us on* - to convince us that we're merely physical beings. We've looked into the mirror created for us, and to varying degrees, accepted the distorted reflection as who we are. *You know it don't you? You've always felt there's much more to life, much more than this, wanting to break out.* But the straightjacket of society, never allowed the time and space to truly experience it; the lightness of you, was always tantalisingly just out of grasp. Well, now there's no longer any reason to be constrained...

It's time to smash the shell into pieces, and emerge pure, in the sunlight, as who you really are.

By this process of Transcendence, using the spiritual compass I've described, all souls can reclaim their divinity. Some will be inspired to ascend into the purely light-based form of Divinicus. Others, who are also evolving along the spiritual path, but require more lifetimes to fully process their karma, will reincarnate in the physical Homo Divinicus form; walking in a more aligned way, with a softer footprint. Clearly, as the Earth's environment condenses down in the 3D, that's going to mean incarnations elsewhere in the cosmos. Which is also something to be embraced with intrigue, mystery and joy, just as with any new incarnation.

Where you go, how you ultimately proceed, will depend on your soul's yearning, and the lessons you have set for yourself to evolve through. Whichever it is, whatever unique path each of us walks, one thing is for sure: as the karmic shell of the old reality steadily breaks down and peels away, it will provide the catalyst - *an enormous impetus and opportunity* - to master this Transcendence. And as painful as it will sometimes be, it is totally necessary, in order for souls to forge a renewed trust in the divine. Not trust that everything will work out in a physical way - you have to wean yourself off this dependency. You have to be able to stare into the mirror of limitation and say... *'I will not be constrained by this smallness anymore. I am much greater than this.'*

This is what's necessary now: for us to rediscover our self respect, by respecting life; to rediscover trust in ourselves, by trusting in the divine; to truly love, by loving ourselves. So now, no matter what happens - *whatever circumstances come our way* - we will have the courage to transcend them, and thus to be secure in our own consciousness: *in the reality of a greater connection, a greater life.*

And so, Divinicus is a divine solution: *a new humanity in a new paradigm.* It represents the next emergence of consciousness, a higher harmony, a higher sense of alignment and joy. Not everyone will have the will nor the commitment required. At this current time, it is only a relative handful in the world who are courageously venturing down the path. We each have to work for it, to fully master ourselves. And how ever challenging it may at times appear to be, I know each of you reading is seeded to master it; you have that configuration and purity in the core of your soul.

You can break through, and reach out...
from the inside.

And when you do, at each twist and turn, you'll find the outstretched hand of the divine awaiting you, rejuvenating and uplifting you; bringing you back into the universal fold.

Like the mystical phoenix, a new humanity will arise through a baptism of fire. But there is nothing to fear. The heat of the flames will serve only to purify and cleanse you. It's time to come together, to reunite as many as possible, as a new humanity, in this new dawning, and to do so by Transcendence, in each and every choice we now make. Because every choice offers the opportunity to be reconnected with the divine once more; to bathe in the fountain of life; to realign and embody soul; to heal broken DNA; reclaim our Original Humanity, and in so doing...

Transform the base metal of Sapiens,
into the shining gold of Divinicus.

CONCLUSION
Back to the Future

It was 29th November 2002. Chris was sitting behind the wheel of a smashed car, obstructing the fast lane of a busy midday motorway, perhaps with only moments to live, yet totally surrendered to his fate. And because of the surrender, something absolutely miraculous happened: wave upon wave of unconditional love flowed down through him... *his spirit-light-body was activating.* The bridge between us was connected. I was able to descend into this realm and into his field. My consciousness helped expand his, until he was flying up in the Fourth Density, taking a review of his life through the images and karmic energy stored there. It's essentially what happens to all people when they pass on. No longer ballasted by mind nor body, your soul floats 'upwards', *inter-dimensionally,* held aloft on the wings of angels. This is where you review everything that's happened to you - what did you learn, what else needs to be achieved? The experience is practically indescribable. The sense of being held and lovingly supported is like returning home after a long and tiring journey, to a place you're totally familiar with - one that accepts you completely, just as you are, without reservation. It's a place of light. It feels like heaven.

Yet Chris' experience was mixed, you could say 'blended'. He'd reviewed his life, but then my consciousness initiated spectacular visions within his light-body field: a premonition of the impelling sense of purpose that drew me here. At the time, I couldn't fully integrate the visions I'd seen, *in this human mind.* Without the journey of rediscovery I've shared in this journal, I couldn't fully comprehend it; a variety of lower consciousness veils, had first to be peeled away. Which is what I put to you now: *you must do likewise, if you are to see the fullness of the multi-dimensional dawning that is now unfolding.*

In essence then, here's what I 'saw' that day, through his 'eyes', and what I'm only now - *after this journey* - fully able to make sense of...

I saw Gaia rising into a new beingness - a New Paradigm - in the Fifth Density. It was a totally new reality at a higher vibrational frequency, positively pulsating with universal life energy. The essence of it was infused with spectacularly vibrant colours, deeply resonant sounds, sense of unity, unconditional love and harmony; the teeming light-being energies of countless physical life forms were dancing in union together.

This new life was steadily emerging and taking form from the ashes of the old, the surface of which I could see transforming: all of the fear-based structures of consciousness on it were fragmenting down. Sophisticated physical life forms were being progressively challenged in this 'fiery crucible' of profound change. There were 'Islands in the Storm' yes, but even these were only temporary; you might consider them 'arks' for the Ascension. Many life forms were ascending through this metamorphosis, including those evolving pioneers of humanity, who would carry the beacon of the human experience - Divinicus - into its next chapter. It was those that had fully heeded the warnings, advice and encouragement by Benevolent Consciousness - they that so cherish mankind and wish for him a more harmonious future.

I saw the consciousness 'skin' of Earth's Fourth Density peeling away, breaking down into a vast, amorphous cloud of energy. I witnessed it being drawn, through time and space, towards the galactic core, to be fragmented into elementals, that it may spawn new life, in a new galaxy, on the other side of the galactic black-hole doorway. Many Earth-bound souls, attached to the previous reality and who could not be recovered, I knew would be fragmented - dissolved back into the Source - in this 'dissolution' process. Sadly, many are just too corrupted - too poisoned - by out-dated behaviours, that their engrossment in the physical means there's practically no way to avoid this dramatic conclusion. As deeply challenging as it is to lose any soul, I now console myself (and others) in the knowing, that even the soul itself, is but a stream of transient experience of the One - the "Seer" of all - which is eternal. The soul can attain immortality, yes, but only through the absolute commitment to self-realisation (in my view, this is often being misunderstood and misinterpreted in the spiritual mainstream).

What of the Opposing Consciousness that had so badly intervened here? It is with great joy, that I could see many of those souls relinquishing the need to control, manipulate and intentionally manifest. As we progress into the future, I see silvery threads reconnecting them to the Source, and their home-coming in other constellations, which will better suit their form and density. But yet, many others I see being drawn into the galactic core and fragmented down - their souls reintegrated with the Source. The elementals of their energy will still carry an imprint of the karmic consciousness that was the manifestation here of the 'Original Mistakes'; so they'll have to play it out again, although ideally in less distorted environments - increasingly aligned states. Progressively, life finds its way back to harmony with the natural flow; it is this continual cleansing, healing and evolving process that will ultimately lead the universe to balanced harmony in all places - to Nirvana.

What of the future for the Earth in the lower physical realm? The Opposing Consciousness had tried everything possible to take ownership, bending the planet to its will, in order to recreate a shadow of its former home: a synthetic reality, more to their desire and vibration - one which they could mercilessly control. Benevolence was never going to let that happen - there would be no negotiation. But for a time, Gaia and her children needed the Intervention too; it provided the intense conditions necessary to process deep-set and dramatic karma. This 'survival-of-the-fittest' reality, is one from which, I can see much has been learned. Paradoxically, it has also spurned some of life's superlative forms. That which caused Gaia unimaginable empathic suffering, also provided the fuel for a more sophisticated evolutionary destiny. So the progressive breaking down of the 3D biosphere I saw causing much transient pain, yes, but also a dynamic crucible of creation, for a greatly enhanced future.

Thus, the old fear-based reality is no longer required by the critical mass of the consciousness that co-created it. And so, through this great purification process, those life forms that had evolved what was required from the old reality, those that would be able to maintain the higher vibrational frequency of being, I saw shedding their redundant forms. The consciousness so liberated, integrated and retained the formless magnificence that it had, over time, evolved. Thus, for me, the tears of sadness quickly gave way to those of joy, as I saw this evolved consciousness taking on all manner of newly enhanced form.

So what now for humanity? In this crucible of profound change, there will be many souls with the capacity to evolve, but who will pass on, without having fully processed their karma. Working tirelessly behind the scenes, starsouls from across the cosmos will help bring them to a safe harbour, in the angelic realms, for a greatly needed period of rest, recuperation and healing, before embarking on a new incarnation, somewhere else in the cosmos; one that can shape and sustain the physical - Homo Divinicus - form; one with realigned DNA; one that will thrive with much greater compassion and softer footprint.

The prospect of this must fill every soul with great optimism. It certainly does mine. I do look forward to the day when, if given, I might walk again on the surface of such a miraculous, bounteous and vibrant planet as this once was: to taste, in a very physical way, the relativistic experience of the illusionary real; so real that it draws you in, and if you're not careful - very mindful of your sentient choices - then disconnects you from God. Collective souls, such as in the animal kingdom, united by a Devic Consciousness, can maintain the balanced and united link. The challenge for a singular soul, is to fully enjoy the bounteous nature of this physical, yet not lose 'himself' in it. That will be the challenge for Homo Divinicus.

And what about Divinicus? Well, 'he' will take on the new light-being form, in the renewed, Fifth Density Earth. It is his immediate destiny to enjoy the 'Garden of Eden' once more - in the New Paradigm; totally interconnected with the bounteous multiplicity of life there. With all sentient forms singing in harmony as one orchestra of interconnected flow. It will be expanded, free, liberating - totally magnificent. For those who've processed their karma and ascended into this new vibration, it will feel just like living in heaven.

And so I was right back at the beginning. I'd ventured out into the universe, and, by the Law of Attraction working to figure out distortion, I'd lost myself in another soul's body, one which was deeply resonant with mine. I'd been drawn here because of my awareness and understanding of such Opposing Consciousness Intervention, elsewhere in the cosmos. Yet just like others incarnating on Earth, I too had to lose myself first, in order to find myself again, and thereby fully empathise with the very complex and challenging situation we face here right now. Conversely, like many souls on Earth at the moment, it was Chris' yearning to ascend out of the mayhem, and move into a higher harmony of balance and alignment - *the new Divinicus*. Thus we helped each other. It was our sacred agreement.

In many ways, as difficult as it may be to swallow, all of mankind has had a similar sacred agreement with the entities of the Intervention. Right at the beginning of the universe, as the One became self-aware, and then began to lose itself in the illusion of separation, a karmic dynamic was created. Eddy currents of manifestation formed: swirls of density, caused by lack of awareness; the subtle desire to control the flow; 'Revelling in Physicality'; or else it was the 'Pain of Existence' - being temporarily lost in the relativistic background noise of the universe. Of course they're all distortions, of the bounteous wonder of life itself, the other side of the coin. But at those higher dimensions, each glitch in the flow of self-realisation, manifests at the speed of thought. The manifestation then cascades downwards, through the densities, taking on various forms of reality, which must be played out to resolve the distortion.

Thus, these Original Mistakes, created a wide variety of different situations, in many different places, with different 'protagonists' - *actors in the drama of life.* And because each actor is a manifestation of the One's own self-confusion, working to find the higher harmony again, so each soul has 'agreed' to be here - to experience the Intervention, but then unravel itself: to ditch the karmic baggage; attain a new level of mastery; *sense once more the fullness of a loving heart, and ascend into a higher vibration - the New Paradigm.* Thus, we taste the relativistic sweetness of life itself.

Even Gaia herself, has had a similar karmic distortion to play out. During the early formation of our solar system, she could not endure the intense compaction of her devic soul into an early protoplanet. Yet again, this event was playing out the Pain of Existence: unity consciousness was locked into the immense torsional density, as the planet was forming, and thereby suffering from the apparent isolation from the Source. Before the veils of separation are peeled away, such polarity can cause immense stress. In a human, that might result in a condition like cancer; in a planet, it can literally tear the materiality apart. And so it did, forming the asteroid belt we now witness between Mars and Jupiter.

And thus, Gaia drew to herself the controlling matrix of energy, that has so devastated her once green and beautiful land. She needed it to experience the karmic pain: to accept it, and then to more gradually release herself from identification with it. Ultimately, by this complex and comprehensive self-realisation process, she'd manifest a spectacular new form, rejuvenated in all her heavenly glory.

So Gaia needed her rebellious and unruly children too. She needed those that would control, disrespect and trash her Earth's surface. But what a 'plan', what a realisation - that those warring children from the faraway reaches of the cosmos, from different cultures, creeds and even species, might one day embody in the same *human form*. Different but related souls, with a universe of divergent experience, would all merge together, in one heavenly body. It's masterful. You're left with no choice: you have to see past that which separates us, and harmonise instead, with that which unites us...

Brothers and sisters from all walks of life,
from all places in the cosmos,
must now come together to seal our divine destiny.

For the challenges that we now face together, there is no one to blame. It is simply the universe unravelling eddy currents - distortions - in the flow. *But we are responsible for what now happens.* By coming together, in self-sustaining and supportive communities, we have the capacity to make the unwinding process of this Great Realignment more manageable. This now, is surely the collective yearning within the soul of man: to be connected to the Source once more; aligned with the flow and unburdened by lower distortion; to be enlightened; to live life as a bountiful expression of the One. And this is exactly what the next evolution of mankind is designed to be: a divine being, living a divine life - "Divinicus" - your divine destiny.

So be patient - and persistent - my dear friends,
for all will surely come!

Openhand Foundation

Purpose
The purpose of Openhand is to catalyse Spiritual Evolution by helping people dissolve conditioned behaviour patterns and limiting beliefs. In this way, Openhand empowers people to find their true beingness and ascend into a magical new reality based on unconditional love, joy and unity with all life.

Not for profit
Openhand is a not for profit organisation. Which means we do not have shareholders and no member benefits by taking profit. All surplus revenue is reinvested to facilitate our objective - to help others through the process of Ascension.

Worldwide Seminars, Workshops and Courses
We are given to spread the message and visions contained within this book as far and wide as possible. In line with this calling, we conduct seminars, courses, workshops and retreats around the globe. If you would like us to run a seminar or course for your organisation or private group, email courses@Openhandweb.org

Join our growing community
Here at Openhand, it brings great joy to our hearts to witness the miraculous expansion of consciousness taking place across our planet. It is within our purpose to join together a virtual community of ascending people to share advice, resources, transformational tools, philosophy and above all, a common bond of unconditional love. Our website provides a platform for this growing community. To find out more about Openhand, visit...

www.Openhandweb.org

Five Gateways: Our Journey of Ascension

There are many ways up the 'spiritual mountain', for each of us there is a unique path; yet those who have climbed before us often speak of five key expansions, five key 'altitudes' through which we all tend to pass. It is a common journey that has been followed by spiritual masters through the ages.

Trinity's Conscious Kitchen

The official Openhand recipe book, designed to inspire soul through compassionate and conscious cuisine. In the spirit of raising our consciousness, all recipes are original, animal-free, wheat-free and free from refined sugar. Most people who eat this way not only experience optimal health, but also greater spiritual, mental and emotional clarity.

"**5 Gateways**" is a powerful Openhand documentary, detailing from direct first hand experience, the spiritual transitions we all must make if we are to peel away the blockages that limit us and unfold into the new paradigm.

The time is now. There is no other time!

For Guided Meditations to help in your evolution, and all publications above, visit our web community: www.Openhandweb.org

"There is a natural flow
through all events and
circumstances in our lives,
just like a stream flowing
down the mountain.

To be in perfect harmony
is to align with this flow,
and in order to do so,
we must first release.

Let go. Open your hand!"

Lightning Source UK Ltd.
Milton Keynes UK
UKOW02f0027080716

277931UK00002B/319/P